The Revolt of the Masses

The Revolt of the Masses

by
JOSÉ ORTEGA Y GASSET

Translated, Annotated, and with an Introduction by
Anthony Kerrigan
Edited by Kenneth Moore
With a Foreword by Saul Bellow

University of Notre Dame Press
Notre Dame, Indiana

Cloth edition published 1985 by
University of Notre Dame Press,
Notre Dame, Indiana

Foreword copyright © 1985 by
Saul Bellow

Introduction copyright © 1985 by
Anthony Kerrigan

Illustrations copyright © 1985 by
Douglas Kinsey

Copyright © 1985 by
W. W. Norton & Co.

Library of Congress Cataloging in Publication Data

Ortega y Gasset, José, 1883-1955.
The revolt of the masses.

Translation of: La rebelión de las masas.
1. Civilization.   2. Proletariat.   3. Europe—
Civilization.   I. Moore, Kenneth, 1930-
II. Title.
CB103.0713   1985   901   81-40457
ISBN 0-268-01609-7

Manufactured in the United States of America

Contents

Acknowledgments

THE PREPARATION of this volume was made possible, initially, by a grant from the Weil Centrifugal Pump Company, in memory of Ralph David Weil, founder.

Grants followed from the MacArthur Foundation, the Wilbur Foundation, the Earhart Foundation, and the Joyce Foundation. The National Endowment for the Arts allocated funds, and the National Endowment for the Humanities was repeatedly supportive in underwriting the translation of three volumes: the present volume and two additional volumes of Ortega's writings; the last two are not yet scheduled for publication. For his liaison backing, thanks are due to Dr. David C. Leege, Director of the Center for the Study of Man in Contemporary Society, University of Notre Dame. The polemical and ghostly Dr. (St. Andrews, Scotland) Russell Kirk contributed materially as well as spiritually. The novelist William O'Rourke recast several paragraphs in the opening texts and made stylistic changes. Professor Angel Delgado promoted retention of certain controversial passages of an anti-popular nature in the Introduction. The polymath Dr. Denis Goulet focused attention on the French thinker Gabriel Marcel's reaction to Ortega. The poet Jeanne Cook carried out fruitful work on the entire manuscript. Richard Allen, editor of the printed text, made subtle improvements and displayed Aristotelian flair.

Foreword

SAUL BELLOW

WHAT A MASS MAN is, Ortega amply and indeed elegantly defines for us in Anthony Kerrigan's superb translation of *La rebelión de las masas*, but a rapid sketch of the argument of the book may nevertheless be useful to the reader.

Ortega when he speaks of the mass man does not refer to the proletariat; he does not mean us to think of any social class whatever. To him the mass man is an altogether new human type. Lawyers in the courtroom, judges on the bench, surgeons bending over anaesthetized patients, international bankers, men of science, millionaires in their private jets are, despite their education, their wealth, or their power, almost invariably mass men, differing in no important respect from TV repair men, clerks in Army-Navy stores, municipal fire-inspectors, or bartenders. It is Ortega's view that we in the West live under a dictatorship of the commonplace. The triumphs of science and technology have made possible a huge increase in population, and with new multitudes has come a revolutionary change in the character of civilized society, for in Ortega's view revolution is not merely an uprising against the existing institutions but the establishment of a new order which reverses traditional order. The modern revolution has created for the average man, for the great social conglomerate to which he now belongs, a state of mind radically opposite to the old. Public life has been turned inside out. The unqualified individual, "equal in law," belongs to the sovereign mass. Examining the collective assumptions of this sovereign mass Ortega reaches the conclusion that, although the world remains in certain respects civilized, its inhabitants are barbarians. In Ortega's view barbarism is defined by the absence of norms. "There is no culture where there are no principles of civil legality to which to appeal." In mass society philosophy and art suffer the same fate as the legal traditions.

What are the characteristics of Ortega's mass man? He is unable to distinguish between the natural and the artificial. Technology, which surrounds him with cheap and abundant goods and services, with packaged bread, subways, blue-jeans, with running water and electrical fixtures that light up at the touch of a finger, has as it were worked itself into his mind as an extension of the natural world. He expects that there will be air to breathe, sunlight. He also expects elevators to go up, buses to arrive. His ability to distinguish between artifact and organism withers away. Blind to the miraculous character of nature, as well as to the genius of technology, he takes both for granted. So in Ortega's mass society the plebeians have conquered, and they do not concern themselves with civilization as such but only with the wealth and conveniences provided by mechanization. The spirit of a mass society bids it to abandon itself freely to itself and to embrace itself; practically nothing is impossible, nothing is dangerous and, in principle, no one is superior to anyone else—this, Ortega submits, is the mass man's creed. The "select man" by contrast, insofar as he serves a transcendental purpose, understands that he must accept a kind of servitude. "To live at ease," said Goethe, "is plebeian; the noble mind aspires to ordinance and law." It follows from this that the mass man lacks seriousness. With him nothing is for real, all parts are interchangeable. For him everything is provisional. He may occasionally play at tragedy, but the prevailing mood is one of farce. The mass man loves gags. He is a spoilt child, demanding amusement, given to tantrums, lacking the form, the indispensable tension which only imperatives can give. His only commandment is Thou shalt expect convenience. "The only real effort is expended in fleeing from one's own destiny."

And what, according to Ortega, is the destiny of this barbarian? The opening up of life and the world for the mediocre man has led him to shut up his soul. It is the obliteration of the average soul upon which the rebellion of the masses is founded. "Which, in turn, constitutes the gigantic problem facing humanity today." How the soul is going to react to this, or whether it is going to react, Ortega does not tell us in this book. He takes the matter up elsewhere. In *Man and People* he discusses the psychic struggle of the individual self and the necessity of "being inside oneself" as a prerequisite for the formation of true ideas, for the gestation of those original and creative actions without which societies die.

"The rebellion of the masses is one and the same thing as the fabulous increase in the standard of living in modern times. But the reverse side of this phenomenon is fearsome: the rebellion of the masses represents a radical demoralization of humanity." This is Ortega at his most pessimistic. True, he says, the level attained in the West is superior to any in the past as far as the average man is concerned, but if we look to the future we find grounds to fear that it will neither preserve this level nor reach a higher one. "On the contrary, it may well regress to inferior levels." In the sphere of politics he seems to take it for granted that the masses act through the state, and that under the dominion of the masses the state will inevitably crush the independence of the individual.

I think it only fair to point out that the circumstances of the West are vastly different to what they were when this book was first published. Ortega is writing about the West's honeymoon with technology. That honeymoon ended decades ago. Doubts and fears obviously pervade mass society.

Although the standard of living has continued to rise, the
confidence of modern man has been greatly shaken by the
mounting crisis of civilization, by wars and by the speed of
change, by the mass man's gradual recognition that the world's
resources are after all finite. Besides, the masses do not after
all dominate the state. It cannot be said that sophisticated
police states express the will of their masses, or that Hitler or
Stalin led nations of spoilt children in World War II. Nor do
the mass media reflect the dominion of the masses; they demonstrate instead the skill of the illusionists who form public
opinion and public taste. The average man cannot think that
he understands or controls what is happening. He is unable
to believe confidently in the explanatory pictures he is shown.
Vulgarity in the eighties is not as sure of itself as it was fifty
years ago. Crisis has chastened it considerably. If humanity
today is demoralized, the cause is perhaps not to be sought
in the rebellion of the masses but in the setbacks suffered by
mass society, in the thickening shadow of its all too realistic
fears, above all in the pain felt by the hounded, mutilated,
not wholly obliterated soul.

Ortega, to be sure, had his ancestors. Earlier writers,
Nietzsche among them, had announced with revulsion the
advent of a new human type (in *Zarathustra* Nietzsche calls
him the "Last Man"), but Ortega is in no sense a derivative
thinker. Ortega's mass man is descended from the bourgeois
as the nineteenth century artist saw him—Stendhal's small
businessmen and provincial political types, Flaubert's Homais,
Dostoievsky's worshippers of Baal. These writers are among
Ortega's predecessors, and he sees the twentieth century, in
part, from their perspective: a diminished and fatally dis-
figured human type, a new force in the world numbering
hundreds of millions of individuals has come to dominate
modern civilization.

One has only to read a single page of Ortega to see that
he is entirely his own man. He has read widely but he im-
itates no one. The French writer David Mata has recently said

of him that he is "a source, a spring. He is so unpedantic, so unbombastic that he is barely a traditional philosopher at all: he seems so transparent that he is nothing, nothing but light. On any theme he ponders . . . he sheds a noonday brightness in which prejudices, idols of the tribe, entelechies, all dissolve" (*Encounter*, Feb. 1982). And although he is a civilized European, *un grand Européen*, his light is uniquely Spanish.

SAUL BELLOW

Introduction

ORTEGA, AS HE IS most simply known in Spanish, was born at the time of Victoria in England, a deliberately, almost advisedly benighted time which in retrospect seems halcyon. A few years before his birth a Spanish student at Sandhurst, England's Royal Military College, was summoned to the throne of Spain as Alfonso XII. The times were not frenetic, and neither were they heroic. Ortega grew up in Madrid and Andalucía, the son and grandson of leading figures in the world of journalism: his grandfather was founder of a large daily in Madrid, his father the director of a prestigious literary review. Withal, Ortega found his Spain stifling, *achabacanado*, mediocre and vulgar, and, after obtaining his doctorate in Madrid (with a thesis titled "The Terrors of the Year One Thousand"), he fled, "like a medieval scholar" (he was a Latinist and Hellenist), to Leipzig, "famous for its universities and bookstores," in his words. The *peseta* was so near-valueless that his state-grant allowed meals only irregularly. In Germany he breathed philosophy: Nietzsche and other moving spirits. A dominant personal influence was that of Hermann Cohen, the neo-Kantian. It was not Ortega's last stay in Germany, and he remained close to German thought all his life.[1]

While Ortega was in his teens, there was an acceleration in the decline of empire. Two years before the end of the nineteenth century, the Spanish-American War led to the loss of Cuba and the Philippines, and Spain sank to the point where "it lost its pulse," in the words of the conservative statesman Francisco Silvela, author of *El mal gusto literario en el siglo XVIII* (*The Literary Bad Taste of the Eighteenth Century*). Revolution was expected, but the populace went to the bull-fight instead. The intellectuals of the so-called "Generation of '98" (1898 being the year Spain lost the last of its empire) were crystalized by the disaster. New values were sought for Spain.

In the book he entitled *La rebelión de las masas*, José Ortega y Gasset produced a masterwork of philosophical sociology. A variant description of his investigations as a whole is that he plumbed the human psyche like a *metaphysical* anthropologist.[2] The present work is also a "metaphysics of history," as the author himself suggests when he ironically eschews that very notion (while noting that he is "clearly constructing one") at the beginning of Chapter 9.

  In accordance with the Library of Congress cataloguing system, Ortega's works are classified under the general heading of "Auxiliary Sciences of History," placing him on the same shelf with another historical metaphysician, Oswald Spengler and *The Decline of the West*, a book Ortega closely read, refuted—and whose *Zeitgeist* he shared.

  By whatever standards, this book has become a classic. Like many classics, especially Spanish ones, it is merely an exercise in the obsessive freedom to think "in a manner of speaking." (The various chapters, moreover, are each an individual lecture in a series.) Another great Spanish writer, Cervantes, produced his classic with the freedom of genius. Cervantes had more or less unwittingly (irresponsibly perhaps) postulated his Spain on two levels, apparent in the dissimilar "circumstances" of his two leading characters. He was thought to have mocked the anachronism of chivalry in a nonchivalric age, but he wrote in romantic terms, and he did anything but denigrate or destroy eternal romance.

  As regards classics, Ortega believed "There is but one way

to salvage a classic: to give up reverence and to use it for our own un-salvaged salvation, to lay aside its status as a classic, to make it contemporary. Its pulse must rebound from an infusion of our own blood." This introductory note is devoted to paraphrasing and updating the terms of Ortega's classic.

Ortega described a societal phenomenon around him, and also—not as unwittingly (or as irresponsibly) as Cervantes, but most pointedly—he diagnosed mass society as it exists particularly in the Western world today. His diagnosis continues valid, ever more so, despite the emendations of time—which only serve to confirm his clinical observations and make them more pertinent than ever, because the disease he diagnosed has spread and become more virulent.

Ortega's germane predecessor in Spain, Miguel de Unamuno is the best-known internationally of the "Generation of '98." It is clear only now that he was Ortega's chief antipode, and the two are seen to be the two poles of Spanish thought in the last hundred years. At this date, a glance at the parallels between these two looming figures proves more rewarding than a chronological survey of Ortega's subsequent life and evolving philosophy. One grew out of the other, and both, seen from this distance, were opposite faces of the same Spanish coin, and between them summarize Spanish thought in the twentieth century.

Unamuno, the Prophet of Uncertainty, is universally known for *The Tragic Sense of Life*, and best known in the United States, England, and Ireland for the seven volumes translated and published under the auspices of the Bollingen Foundation (Bollingen Series LXXXV: Princeton University Press, 1967-1984). Volumes 3 through 7 incorporate his chief work: *The Agony of Christianity*, along with *The Tragic Sense of Life*, and such key stories as "Saint Manuel Bueno, Martyr." (The first two volumes in the series are marked by such tergiversation in the editing that they are outside the canon.)

Ortega is well-known in the English-speaking world through good and bad translations.

Both Spaniards were alien to fashionable European rationalism, and each held to his own brand of "vitalism." Unamuno's was pointedly irrationalist. And he supplied irrationalism with "its most forceful, intense, impassioned and effective formulation" (in the words of Julián Marías, Unamuno and Ortega scholar), when he loosed a definition to toll down the ages: "To live is one thing and to know is another. . . . Perhaps between them there is such an opposition that we can say *whatever is vital is antirational — and not merely irrational — and whatever is rational is antivital.* And that is the basis of the tragic sense of life." Reason is the enemy of life, for it tends toward death the way memory tends toward stability, and the living individual being, moreover, is strictly unintelligible. Logic requires an *identical type* in any place or time, while in fact there is nothing which remains the same for two successive moments of its being. The idea of God is different each time He is conceived. To analyze is to stop a thing, to deprive it of life, to kill it. The combat of life with reason is a tragic combat, the basis of tragedy. Thereupon, Unamuno concludes: "Reason is not vital."

Whereupon, Ortega stands Unamuno's conclusion on its head and enunciates his famed concept of "vital reason." Neither irrationalism nor rationalism! Neither idealism nor materialism! Neither abstract absolutism nor skeptical relativism! Reason is lived, much as is the sense of sight or touch. Since reason is a given in the course of life it must perforce be vital.

While he was still studying in Germany, Ortega was already in correspondence with his elder, Unamuno, and, in speaking of the nature of the novel, he announced that he held Cervantes to be "the only Spanish philosopher." That is, Cervantes philosophized directly from life, he created a *living* philosophy as lived in the course of adventures which allowed his hero to be himself, the man Don Quixote. To be heroic is to want to be heroic. Both Ortega and Unamuno agreed on the heroic Don Quixote: Only such a hero can say "I know who I am," for to be is to want to be something. To be a hero is to want to be oneself, which is an act of will.

But: Don Quixote is fictional? So perhaps are his fictive readers. Jorge Luis Borges, who is intellectually linked directly with Unamuno (Borges also sent Unamuno his own early books and corresponded with him), has often suggested that man is a dream, Someone Else's fiction. It is an old theme in Spanish literature, from Calderon's *Life is a Dream* to Unamuno's "Nivolas," or "Fictions" (Borges issued a book titled *Ficciones*), in which Unamuno challenges his readers, questioning whether their existence is in fact any more "real" than that of the characters being read about. Borges has gone a step farther in his "The Circular Ruins," where the main character dreams a man into existence, only to realize that he himself is someone else's dream.

For Unamuno and even more for Ortega, man is what he does. He is himself—and his circumambience, his particular set of circumstances. Ortega's single most characteristic phrase is *"Yo soy yo y mi circunstancia"*: "I am myself and my circumstance." (At first, Ortega had used *horizonte*: horizon: "I am myself and my horizon.") Life, not thought, is the point of departure. Ortega's dictum is fundamental to his descriptive ontology of human life, its being and reality. The *I* cannot think of itself without thinking of its own circumstances, and it cannot think of its circumstance without thinking of itself as the dynamic center of them.

Before there was a body of existential writing in France or Germany, both Unamuno and Ortega had felt that life is an encounter and dialogue with reality. What is done with one's life is the only destiny. Reality for man is reality-as-such plus himself as its discoverer. For Manuel Durán, a perceptive Orteguian scholar in America, Ortega is saying that "man is not a thing, not even a 'be-ing,' but an occurrence, what comes to pass. . . . Life itself is a 'be-ing' which creates itself" (*Or-*

tega y Gasset, 1966, p. 13). In a figure of speech, Ortega says that just as a book is made up of pages, human existence is made up of happenings. Life is an ever-changing and unfinished project. "The only possible rule is that man must strive to discover, repeatedly, his own self, his own vital trajectory, his own profound vocation" (Ibid.).

Paraphrasing Ortega directly, using his own metaphors, we arrive at a dramatic image: Life is like a shipwreck, and we are all castaways. There is an urgent need to act at every moment. We have not chosen either our world or the shipwreck, but we must act to save ourselves. Decisions must be made every moment. Solutions are demanded. Man must choose, elect continually.

In Spanish, the verb "to be" boasts two forms: *ser* and *estar*. The latter represents ephemeral being, what one is at a given moment. It is Ortega's permanent condition — or that of all men, in his philosophy. One must deal with a set of varying circumstances at each moment, and one's being depends on what one does in the shifting circumstances.

Ortega was, precisely because he was "existential," not ever, advisedly, a *systematic* philosopher.

In a tightly-layered book, *Ortega y Gasset, An Outline of his Philosophy* (New Haven, 1957), Jośe Ferrater Mora, a Spanish philosopher in America, succinctly puts the matter in another way, with a Spanish modulation: "Life *happens* to each one of us. It is a pure 'happening' or, as Ortega puts it, a gerundive, a *faciendum*, and not a participle, not a *factum*. Instead of being something 'ready-made', we have to make it unceasingly. Life, in short, is a 'being' that makes itself, or rather 'something' consisting in making itself. . . . The concept of becoming, which some philosophers have propounded as a substitute for the concept of being, is only a trifle more adequate than the latter for the description of human existence. . . . Ortega's philosophy draws nearer to a 'metaphysics of becoming' than to any other type of philosopy" (p. 48)

Ortega spoke of the essential human vocation as "having

to die": one more observation which suggests he fits within the framework of existence philosophy, not to say "existentialist philosophy," even if not precisely matching the marquetry of the disparate school of existentialism as such. It was a demesne in which Unamuno had already been clearly a precursor.

It is worth noting the independent originality which both Spaniards shared. Both were forever at odds with all adherents of abridged thought. They were neither of them welcomed in their maturity by either end of the religious, philosophical, or political spectra. They were both, in sum, unacceptable to either the so-called Right or the so-called Left.

Neither was welcomed by the "Traditionalists," who saw their theory and thought debased in practice by the narrow nationalist victors in the Spanish Civil War (1936-39): and both were out of favor and suffered official disfavor during the rule of Franco, a so-called conservative who managed to conserve almost nothing of the Spanish heritage. When the Republic for which both men had long prepared and which they had always advocated came into being, they were both separately appalled by mob rule. In the end, Unamuno was ousted as Rector of the University of Salamanca, first by the Republic and then by Franco's rebel government, whereupon he gave up the ghost, died, in the first year of the Civil War. That same year, 1936, Ortega left Republican Madrid— walked away from the state he had been instrumental in creating—and went into exile and silence.

"Whenever there is a crowd," wrote Kierkegaard, "there is untruth." Ortega saw—and experienced the crowd's untruth with his five senses. He felt its menace, and that of its iconoclastic mania, a terrible counterforce to the awesome mindlessness of middle-class uniformity.

Unamuno and Ortega spent their lives in conflict with the ready-made, and ironclad, solutions proferred by the futurist Left or the bunkered Right. Both men showed in practice

that they were liberals (of the classic stripe) and conservatives
(also of the classic conserving stripe). They could not, theoretically or organically, make peace with absolutist practi-
tioners of the Liberal dogma or of Conservative profit-taking.
(In their time, Spain boasted a party liberally called *Partido
Liberal-Conservador*.) Neither could identify with any party.
For them, being labelled or pigeonholed according to party
was a treason to their intellectuality.

Ortega had believed that liberalism was one of the highest
aspirations of man, in fact the "noblest," for it was purely a
cultivated goal, the product of high civilization, and thus
"anti-natural," for it made provision for tolerating political
opposition, a consciously developed decision clearly not inherent or instinctive in man.

Ortega was vouching for classic liberalism at all times.
Though he saw that state totalitarianism as he witnessed it
meant death to high-mindedness, and though he foresaw
that democratic totalitarianism would sweep—was sweeping
—the world, he could hardly foresee that the new *Zeitgeist*,
the new belief, which the liberals of the West were already
turning into a dogma of their own, was as intellectually oppressive as old puritanism. At its logical worst, this dogma
would eventuate in these formerly liberal Liberals endlessly
excusing the "people's democracies" and their allies in their
attentats against all freedoms, perpetrated in the name of the
people, in the name of the "masses."

Alien as they were to the twentieth century's worldwide
egalitarian *Zeitgeist*, both Spanish thinkers took as their
point of departure the world as it developed out of Greece
and Rome, through such institutions as the English parliamentary and legal tradition, and the Christian artistic culture
of Europe as a whole. Neither felt a craving for the "primitive," that disease of modern culture, or for moral archaism,
a *nostalgie de la boue*. Unamuno judged that Christianity
was European in practice and final effect and that where it
spread to America it represented Western values. He held to

these values himself, in any case, as did Ortega, who managed never to waste a moment attacking the church. However heterodox, Unamuno was an eschatological thinker. Ortega acted like a classical Roman in his attitude to the popular beliefs of his nation and race: they were his given circumstance. God stood at a great distance from creation (unavailable to charismatics), and Ortega justified theodicy.

In Ortega's day, socialized religion had already made its appearance — anathema to Unamuno, who queried "What is 'social Christianity'?" And added: "We might as well speak of 'blue chemistry'. "

A colorful passage paraphrases Ortega's view: The God of the believer Descartes, inherited from Ockham, "was an awesome and magnificent Being, whose first attribute — most authentic in God, when He is truly God, and not brazenly domesticated, like a lion from Libya or a tiger from Hyrcan — is arbitrariness." (This passage is cited with obvious relish by a Dutch author, J. H. Walgrave, O. P., in a book issued in Spanish translation by *Revista de Occidente*, the publishing house founded by Ortega himself: *La filosofía de Ortega y Gasset*, Madrid, 1965, with Imprimatur "Rector Lovaniensis.")

Man is "divinely discontent," an "amputated being" crying out always to know what is missing in his thought: and therein lies philosophy. Moreover, herein lies the division between masses and select men, as enunciated in the present book. For Ortega accepts Plato's belief that philosophy is the science of free men, of noble men. "Whoever would create — and all creation is aristocratic — must succeed in acting like an aristocrat in the marketplace," added Ortega. And philosophy is the most aristocratic of all activities: a physicist may be a mass-man, but a metaphysicist (*físico/metafísico*) is perforce an aristocrat, by definition. To make philosophy, the most universal and problematic of all ways of knowing, is the most ennobling of occupations, the one which offers dominion over destiny.

In *La rebelión de las masas* we are presented with an incandescent conflict between "the masses" and the select men whose purpose is other than that of the philistines. It should be pointed out at once that the "masses" are not the revolutionary Marxist masses of the so-called "class struggle" (already discredited as a term in Marxist China). They are not even defined here as workers, they are not the proletariat. The mass-man is found on all levels of society, and, in point of fact, Ortega is most concerned with the mentality of mass-men in the upper reaches of society.

Ortega writes: "The division of society . . . is not a division into social classes . . . upper or lower classes." The American writer on social phenomena, the colorful "neologician" Tom Wolfe, examining the surface of the world scene, considers the ankylosis and superannuation of cant words and creeds: "It was impossible to use the word 'proletarian' any longer with a straight face. By the late 1970s the new *masses* began appearing also in France, West Germany, Switzerland, England, Norway, Sweden, Japan . . . which is to say, throughout the *capitalist* world. . . . By 1979 Marxism was finished as a spiritual force, although the idealogues lingered on" ("The Sexed-Up, Doped-Up, Hedonistic Heaven of the Boom-Boom '70s," *Life*, Dec. 1979).

Is the majority itself suspect? Another great Spaniard in America, George Santayana of Harvard, thought so: "The philanthropists are now preparing an absolute subjection of the individual in soul and body to the instincts of the majority—the most cruel and unprogressive of masters; and I am not sure that the liberal maxim 'the greatest happiness of the greatest number,' has not lost whatever was just or generous in its intent" (*George Santayana's America*, J. Ballowe, Chicago, 1967).

Being a classic liberal on principle, Ortega did not inveigh against any majority as such. But often sheer numbers seem to have blurred the distinction between the mass-man (whether he was a rare—and ignorant—specialist or not) and the masses as numbers. Barbarians tend to be plural, a very Woodstock, a veritable Altamont.

Though the "folk" tend to be sound, the "masses" do not. These two distinct words evoke a robust distinction. Ortega wrote essays probing the "aristocratic" nature (in the sense of preservation mostly) of the folk and their lore, and even of their regional dress, in Europe most particularly. How often, in democracies, has not the sound instinct of the folk proven more viable than the elitist machinations of the politicians?

Plato, for his part, felt that the majority of human beings wallow in an ignorance compounded by their ignorance that they are ignorant. This majority, the "masses" in a dictionary sense, is today in the ascendent (along with, but not identical with, mass-man). All political systems in the civilized world are theoretically based on the existence of voters. The modern democracies, unlike those of Greece, bend to the opinion of the majority of voters, a flock which holds trivial pseudo-opinions, and shows a sense of responsibility only to its own narrow self-interests.

The craving for equality can never be satisfied, not with legislation apparently, nor even with universal suffrage. Moreover, no consistent imagination can be expected from the representatives elected by a majority which always favors those who most resemble itself. In one-party states — the entire world of "People's Democracies" — the votes of the individual are carefully made to count for nothing, but a token recognition is given the masses by a stress on the "class origins" of the directing cadres, who ideally (though less and less, as the governing class breeds) should be of humble origin, of lower class provenance. And the very names of all these tyrannies, all called in some way "Democratic" as well as "People's," represent an incantatory bow to the Age of the Common Man, a cynical salute by way of hollow homage to the People, the Masses. On the other hand, the United States of America, not Russia or Communist Poland, is the "workers' paradise." Totalitarian tyrannies stand in confrontation against a tidal wave of totalitarian democracy.

Marshall McLuhan, an imaginative commentator on mass-culture, has pointed out: "The average American worker enjoys amenities for which Croesus, Grassus, the Medici, and Louis XIV would have envied him" (in *Culture is Our Business*, New York, 1970). And the socio-economist Ludwig von Mises concisely reports: "Modern capitalism is essentially mass production for the needs of the masses. The buyers of the products are by and large the same people who as wage earners cooperate in their manufacturing" (*Human Action*, New Haven, 1949).

The masses today bear little resemblance to the oppressed of history. And mass-men with technological power are a new development on the face of the earth.

Ortega's concern, in any case, is not with origins or stations in life, but with attitudes: the attitude of the un-select, of the people with undifferentiated minds and mechanically majoritarian mentality. And the philistine masses, the people who are all "just like everybody else," are today militantly assertive, particularly in the area of democratic totalitarianism, with its plethora of "demands" and myriad "rights." Paradoxically, the majority of mankind is both aggressive in its demands and curiously satisfied with its mental inertia. The ignorant masses of the past paid lipservice, by and large, to the outstanding men of its society. Today there is a popular and well-nurtured suspicion of men and women of quality.

Ortega held that his description of the division in modern society dealt with a "psychological fact." And he held that the rebellion of the masses was a new and unprecedented historical phenomenon.

For if in the past the historical masses may always have brooded on authority and dreamt of freeing themselves of restraint (and not merely of the enormous injustice present in all of man's epochs), they did not have the means or technique of doing so. They could not supplant the hierarchies with themselves. If they revolted from time to time, they quickly gave their allegiance to a new set of leaders from the same ruling caste: they supported one claimant to a throne as against the one holding it. Some mass movements have merely substituted their own leaders for those of the ruling class while the social structure remained unchanged, as in revolutionary Mexico. Under the new totalitarian democracy, the masses themselves form a new and final court of appeal. The mass-man can set — is already setting — the new standards of value. In fact, the values of modern mass-man have been democratically imposed on the world. The masses do not now need to dream of overthrowing authority, they simply continue to usurp the commanding positions. And they have already mentally equated themselves in worth with whomever is nominally above them. More and more they exercise the controls of preference, the function of choice (and of taste, in such things as the media, by means of popularity polls and the "power of the box-office.") They have taken over control from those historical arbiters whom they now consider no better than their equals.

The masses — where they are allowed: certainly not in People's Republics — display a near-congenital lack of mental sphincter-control in the voicing of trivial but militant opinions on any matter whatsoever. Everyone has the right to literacy, especially in "progressive" countries, where state control has expatriated new writing, exiled old classics, and rewritten history, so that the new literates are lethally confronted (as in Rumania or Cuba) with nothing but abysmal propaganda.

The mass-man today feels that he has been perfected by history. He need not be concerned with limitations. Where the masses in the past were limited by lack of means, today the masses around the world have machinery, and technology — and in some benighted ex-colonial countries they are supplied with a promiscuous abundance of machine-pistols to impose their collective will, albeit as interpreted by the state in their name.

There is a radically different way of looking at today's average man in such countries as the United States and Britain: he may not, in historical reality, "really" exist at all. In his last book, one on Spanish literature, (*Lectures on Don Quixote*, New York and London, 1983) the expatriated Russian writer Vladimir Nabokov speaks of the "so-called average man," who is not exactly Ortega's mass-man: "Whether or not his newspaper and a set of senses reduced to five are the main sources of the so-called 'real life' of the so-called average man, one thing is fortunately certain: that the average man himself is but a piece of fiction, a tissue of statistics." In short, the average man is simply the creation of advertising art, of political manipulation: he does not exist as real or "vital" man. That may be, but he is still palpably a menace, even if faceless. And by reason of the twentieth century's new peril, noise—never before such a threat—he is heard. Apart from crowd noise, his personal noise is amplified. For instance, whether in prison yard or university dormitory, his brainless tone-deaf music rocks the walls. To listen in on the air waves, even the international air waves, is to hear, hear in one's viscera, that the mass-man's heart-beat rules the waves. Barbarism is, literally, everywhere.

As to the distinction between "public" and "mass," Marshall McLuhan, the electric-informational-media populist, supplied a novel difference in definition: "Print technology created the public. Electric technology created the mass" (*The Medium is the Massage*, New York, 1967). Ortega could not anticipate the television deluge, so he could scarcely plumb its depths. McLuhan, however, saturating himself in the flood, goes on to declare: "The public, in the sense of a great consensus of separate and distinctive viewpoints is finished." Today the mass audience is successor to the "public."

Is there nothing good to be said for the present rule of the masses? Ortega observed one advantage: the new phenomenon "presents a favorable facet, for it signifies a general rise in the historical level; average existence today moves on a higher plane than it did yesterday." Since he wrote, people get where they are going (where? the Pope gets to Papua, fast and far from Rome) ever faster: there are more automobiles and airplanes that the ones Ortega noted with satisfaction. Food is faster, and the poor can look at the same television non-dramas as the rich—which Ortega could not have suspected—while getting as fat or fatter (no one in the United States is as lean as Don Quixote, the Knight of Leanness, who could make an onion do for a meal). On the other hand, there are also more aspirin variants (than Ortega noted and commended) and more tranquilizers, even in Africa. There are more mental institutions. There is certainly more money. More records are broken, even if there is no greater greatness.

In natural opposition to the mass-man, counterposed to him in the present book—and in the world—is the man who is not a barbarian, not even a "barbarian of erudition and specialization of the type produced by the technological higher learning" (Ortega, in *Mision de la Universidad,* published in 1930, one year after *La rebelión de las masas*). He is the man who forces himself to prove himself—largely to himself. He may be always in the process of proving himself.

The measure of his outward success is secondary. In fact, one need not *be* excellent to belong to the minority, the select minority; one need only harbor special concern for excellence. The man of excellence in matters of civilization is necessarily "noble," whatever his origin. His life is lived in a purposeful intellectual tension, as against the mental inertia of the commonplace man. Where the mass is reactive, he is active (whether he is "active" in the ordinary sense is immaterial, although Ortega suggests a Greek ideal of an athlete in training as paradigm). Whether his ideal projects can be realized or not, the noble-in-practice makes high demands on himself. Doubtless he risks being like Spanish Don Quixote, with consequent mockery. He lives in a self-imposed vassalage, in an "essential servitude: for him, life lacks savor if he does not make it serve some transcendental purpose. And thus he does not find his 'servitude' a form of oppression."

In the original Spanish, Ortega most often uses the adjective "noble" for these select men, but it occurs too frequently for the American ear: in Europe "noble" still sounds noble, but Americans are otherwise conditioned. The select man cultivates his instinct for "noble preferences" (in G. K. Chesterton's terms of definition of man as an animal with such preferences). These select men are not seen to form an elite, as Ortega never tired of repeating in the years after the publication of this book. They are, most simply and naturally, a select *minority*. Ortega's critics, especially the dogmatically "anti-elitist" elitist liberals, have nevertheless persisted in calling him an "elitist."

Marshall McLuhan, an avid reader of Ortega, much taken with the latter's images and distinctions, reduces the argument to a risible level, a perverse *reductio ad absurdum*, when he humorously cites the advertising verbiage put out by a Japanese daily: " 'The foremost newspaper in Japan' beckons to the Western producer: 'Your Japan market is the *Mass Elite*' " (*Culture is Our Business*). This oxymoron, an example of media illiteracy, a bizarre contradiction in terms, is in the nature of a deference to the masses, brought about by the affluence of mass-man, so that even so-called elites are considered mass, a "mass class."

For Ortega, however, the man of "nobility" is an individual answering to his own destiny; he is no member of a group elite, but most simply the man who is impelled by suprapersonal values, by the imperative of superseding himself, never content to be "like everybody else." For the "noble" man, life means — in figures of speech taken from the hunt — to pursue oneself, to find oneself in the covert, to seize or apprehend oneself. Since life is like the hunt, fraught with the perils of the chase, Nietzsche's cry "Live dangerously!" seems a redundancy. Life is a drama of permanent danger in and of itself. More apropos than Nietzsche's summons is the sixteenth century nobleman's commentary *Rien ne m'est sur que la chose incertaine*: "I am certain of nothing but uncertainty."

And, unlike Nietzsche's *Übermensch* at times, the "noble" man is not naturally or necessarily bent on the destruction of the received values of his time and place. "I have accepted the circumstance of my nation and my time," Ortega said on a record cut in 1932 for the *Archivo de la Palabra*. He was far from content with his nation or time, but he planned to build on what he found — and not tear down any edifice or scatter any of the *viejas piedras*, the old stones. Like Oswald Spengler's "Faustian" man, the select man also has an appetite for infinitude. Though he be endowed with a transcendental *I*, he is intimately bound to his circumambience, with which he interacts in vital exuberance, for he is in the closest possible sensual contact with his surrounds and the reality of his senses. And still, this active man has transcendental limitations. He controls his destiny precisely because he is aware that "the enigma of the universe is insoluble." Of this finite knowledge he makes a strength.

The text used in the translation is the definitive, revised edition of *La rebelión de las masas*, ed. Paulino Garagorri (Madrid: Revista de Occidente en Alianza Editorial, 1979), corrected by hand for our use by the editor.

Anthony Kerrigan
Notre Dame, Indiana 1984

Part I
THE REVOLT OF THE MASSES

1

The Crowd Phenomenon*

THE MOST IMPORTANT FACT in the public life of the West[1] in modern times, for good or ill, is the appearance of the masses in the seats of highest social power. Since the masses, by definition, neither can nor should direct their own existence, let alone that of society as a whole, this new development means that we are now undergoing the most profound crisis which can afflict peoples, nations, or cultures. Such a crisis has occurred more than once in history. Its physiognomy, its outline and profile, and its consequences are known, and the development can be given a name: the rebellion of the masses.

In order to understand this truly formidable phenomenon, we had best avoid the exclusively or primarily political meanings of the words "rebellion," "masses," and "social power." For public life is not only political, but is equally, and even more so, economic, moral, intellectual, and religious. It includes all our collective habits, even our fashions in dress and modes of amusement.

* I have also dealt with the theme that this essay develops in my book *España invertebrada*, published in 1921, in an article in *El Sol*, entitled "Masas" (1926), and in two lectures before the Association of the Friends of Art in Buenos Aires (in 1928). My purpose now is to review and complete what I have already said so that the result will be an organic doctrine on the most crucial fact of our time.

[Asterisks indicate Ortega's footnotes, superscript numbers editorial notes. The latter are gathered at the end of the text.]

Perhaps the best way of approaching this historical phenomenon is to rely on our visual experience: we can simply look at this aspect of our epoch as it stands plainly before our eyes.

Most simple to enunciate, and not so easy to analyze: I shall call it the phenomenon of agglomeration, of crowding, of the sign which says "Full." The cities are full of people. The houses are full of tenants. The hotels are full of guests. Public transport is full of passengers. The cafes and restaurants are full of customers. The sidewalks are full of pedestrians. The waiting-rooms of famous doctors are full of patients. Public spectacles, unless they be extemporaneous, and public entertainment halls, unless they be minoritarian and experimental, are full of spectators. The beaches are crowded, full. What previously was not a problem, is now an everyday matter: the search—to find room, to find a place, to find space.

Is there any fact simpler, more obvious, more constant in life today? Let us penetrate beneath this superficial observation. We will then be surprised to see how, unexpectedly, a veritable fountain will spout forth, and in it, in this jet, we will see how, in the white light of day, of this very day, it will break down into its rich spectrum of inner colors.

What do we actually see, and in seeing are surprised? We see the multitude as such in possession of the locales and appurtenances created by civilization. Further reflection will make us surprised at our surprise. Is not this plenitude ideal? A theater's seats are made to be occupied by spectators: it should be full. And the same for public transport and hotel rooms. No doubt about it. But the point is that previously none of these establishments and vehicles were full—and now they are overflowing, with people left outside eager to occupy them all. Though this development is natural and even logical, we know this was not the case before. A change, therefore, has taken place. Something new has been added, and this innovation does, at least initially, justify our surprise.

To be surprised, to wonder, is to begin to understand. It is the sport and special pleasure of intellectual man. The specific trade-mark of his guild is to gaze at the world with the wide-open eyes of wonder. The world is always strange and wonderful for wide-open eyes. This faculty of wide-eyed wonder is a delight unavailable to your ordinary football or soccer fan. The man who lives by his intellect goes about the world in the perpetual intoxication of a visionary. His particular attribute: the eyes of wonder, of amazement. Thus the ancients assigned to Minerva an owl, bird of wide open ever-dazzled eyes.[2]

Crowding was not a common feature of the past. Everything was not always full. Why is it now?

The members of this ubiquitous mass have not come from out of the blue. The number of people was constant for a good while; moreover, after any war one would expect the number to decrease. But here we come up against the first important modern factor. The individuals who make up the present mass already existed before — but not as a mass, not as "masses." Scattered about the world in small groups, or even alone, they lived in diverse ways, dissociated and distant from one another. Each group, even each individual, occupied a space, each his own space so to say, in the fields, in a village, a town, or even in some quarter of a big city.

Now, suddenly, they appear on the scene as a mass. Wherever we look we see a concentration, masses. *Wherever?* No; more exactly in the places most in demand, the places created by the relatively sophisticated taste of modern culture, places previously reserved for small groups, for select minorities.

The masses, suddenly, have made themselves visible, and have installed themselves in the preferred places of society. In the past, the mass, where it existed, went unnoticed. It was a background to the social scene, to the stage of society. Now it has advanced to the footlights, and plays the part of the leading character. There are no longer protagonists as such: there is only the chorus.

The concept of the masses is quantitative — and visual. Let us translate it, without alteration, into sociological terms. We then encounter the concept of the social mass. Society is always a dynamic unity composed of two factors: masses and minorities. The latter are comprised of especially qualified individuals and groups. The masses are made up of persons not especially qualified. By masses, we do not therefore mean, either simply or even principally, the "working class," the working masses as a whole. The mass is the "average man." Thus, the merely quantitative — the multitude, the mass — becomes a qualitative determinant: it is the common quality, the social animal as stray, man in the measure in which he is undifferentiated from other men, man repeating in himself a generic type. What gain is there is this conversion of quantity into quality? Simply this: by means of quality, we can understand the genesis of quantity. It is as obvious as a platitude that the normal formation of a mass, a multitude, is based on a coincidence of desires, of ideas, of manners among the individuals who compose it. It may be pointed out that precisely the same happens in regard to any social group, however select it may claim to be. True enough: but an essential difference exists.

In those groups which are neither mass nor multitude, the effective cohesion of the members is based on some desire, idea, or ideal, which in itself alone excludes the majority of people. In order to form a minority — of whatever kind it may be — it is first of all necessary that each member separate himself from the multitude for some *special*, relatively personal, reason. His agreement with the others who form the minority is, therefore, secondary, posterior to having adopted an individual attitude, having made himself *singular*; therefore, there is an agreement not to agree with others, a coincidence in not coinciding. A vivid example of this singularity is to be found in the case of the English Nonconformists: they concurred with each other only on their disconformity with the infinite multitude of others. This formation of a minority precisely in order to separate itself from the majority is a basic impulse. The poet Mallarmé, apropos of the select audience at a recital by a distinguished musician, wittily remarked that by the scarcity of its presence the audience was emphasizing the absence of the multitude.

In all truth, the masses, any mass, can make its presence felt as a psychological fact without the need for individuals to appear in agglomeration. We can tell a mass-man when we see one: one person can represent a mass phenomenon. The mass-man is anyone who does not value himself, for good or ill, by any particular criterion, and who says instead that he is "just like everybody else." Despite this ridiculous claim, he will not feel any disquiet, but rather feel reassured, smugly at ease, to be considered identical with all others. A truly humble man who attempts to evaluate his specific worth, and tries to find if he possesses any talent, or excels in any way, may discover in the end that he is endowed with no remarkable qualities, and may conclude that he is ungifted and depressingly ordinary. But he may still consider that he is not part of the mass, not in his own self a mass-man.

In speaking of "select minorities," universal misunderstanding holds sway and manages as usual to distort the meaning, and to ignore the fact that the select individual is not the petulant snob who thinks he is superior to others, but is, rather, the person who demands more from himself than do others, even when these demands are unattainable. For undoubtedly the most radical division to be made of humanity is between two types:[3] those who demand much of themselves and assign themselves great tasks and duties, and those who demand nothing in particular of themselves, for whom living is to be at all times what they already are, without any effort at perfection — buoys floating on the waves.

I am here reminded that orthodox Buddhism is composed of two distinct religions: one, more strict and difficult, the other more lax and easy: the Mahayana, the "great vehicle" or "great way," and the Hinayana, the "lesser vehicle," or "lesser way." The decisive difference lies in choosing one or the other vehicle, in making a maximum of demands on oneself or a minimum.

The division of society into masses and select minorities is not, then, a division into social classes, but into two kinds of men, and it does not depend on hierarchically superior or inferior classes, on upper classes or lower classes. Of course it is plain enough that among the superior classes, when they genuinely achieve this status and maintain it, there is more likelihood of finding men who choose the "great vehicle," while the inferior are those who normally are not concerned with quality. Strictly speaking, there are "masses" and minorities at all levels of society—within every social class. A characteristic of our times is the predominance, even in those groups who were traditionally selective, of mass and popular vulgarity. Even in intellectual life, which by its very essence assumes and requires certain qualifications, we see the progressive triumph of pseudo-intellectuals—unqualified, unqualifiable, and, in their own context, disqualified. The same holds true for the remnants of the nobility, whether male or female. On the other hand, it is not unusual to find among workers, who formerly might have served as the best example of the "mass," outstandingly disciplined minds and souls.

Then there are activities in society which by their very nature call for qualifications: activities and functions of the most diverse order which are special and cannot be carried out without special talent. Thus: artistic and aesthetic enterprises; the functioning of government; political judgment on public matters. Previously these special activities were in the hands of qualified minorities, or those alleged to be qualified. The masses did not try or aspire to intervene: they reckoned that if they did, they must acquire those special graces, and must cease being part of the mass.[4] They knew their role well enough in a dynamic and functioning social order.

If we now revert to the assumptions made at the beginning, the facts will appear as clearly heralding a changed mass attitude. Everything indicates that the "public," that is, the mass,[5] along with wielding power, has decided to occupy the foreground of social life, as well as the front-row seats, and to avail themselves of the pleasures formerly reserved for the few. It is obvious that those seats were never intended for the masses, for they are limited in number; so now there is crowding, making clear to the eye, with visible language, that a new phenomenon exists: the mass, without ceasing to be mass, supplants the minorities.

No one, I believe, begrudges the public's enjoying themselves in greater number and measure than before, since they now have the desire and the means to do so. The only resultant wrong is that the determination of the masses to usurp the place of the minority does not and cannot confine itself to the arena of pleasure alone, but is a generalized practice of the times. And thus (to anticipate what we shall see later), it seems to me that recent political innovations signify nothing less than the political reign of the masses. Western democracy was formerly tempered by a large dash of liberalism and by a ritual trust in the law. In serving these principled ideas the individual bound himself to maintain some discipline in himself. Minorities could take refuge and find support in liberal principles and the judicial norm. Democracy and law (life in common under the law) were synonymous. Today we witness the triumph of hyperdemocracy in which the mass takes direct action oblivious of the law, imposing its own desires and tastes by material pressure. It is false to say that the masses have grown weary of politics and have handed over its operation to selected people. Exactly the opposite is true.

That is what used to happen: that was liberal democracy. The masses took it for granted that, after all, and despite the defects and faults of the select minorities, these minorities understood something more of political problems than they themselves did. Nowadays the mass believes it has the right to impose and lend force to notions deriving from its own platitudes. I doubt that any previous epoch of history has seen such direct government by the multitude as is current in our time. Thus I speak of hyperdemocracy.

The same happens in other orders of life, particularly in the intellectual order. I may be mistaken, but it seems that the writer nowadays, whenever he assumes the task of saying anything on any subject to which he has given thought, must bear in mind that the average reader, who has never pondered the matter—and always assuming that he reads the writer at all—does not read in order to learn anything, but rather reads him in order to pronounce judgment on whether or not the writer's ideas coincide with the pedestrian and commonplace notions the reader already carries in his head. If the individuals who make up the mass thought of themselves as specially qualified, we would have on our hands merely a case of personal error, not a matter of sociological subversion. *The characteristic note of our time is the dire truth that the mediocre soul, the commonplace mind, knowing itself to be mediocre, has the gall to assert its right to mediocrity, and goes on to impose itself wherever it can.* In the United States it is considered indecent to be different. The mass crushes everything different, everything outstanding, excellent, individual, select, and choice. Everybody who is not like everybody else, who does not think like everybody else, runs the risk of being eliminated. Of course "everybody else" is not *everybody*. In normal times, "everybody" was the complex union of mass with special, divergent minorities. Today, "everybody" means the mass, the masses—and only the masses.[6]

2

The Rise of the Historic Level

Such, then, is the formidable phenomenon of our time, which we have described without hiding the brutality of its features. This phenomenon is, moreover, unprecedented in the history of our civilization. Nothing like it has ever appeared in the course of our modern evolution. If we are to find its like, we must take a leap outside our history and immerse ourselves in a different element, a vital world altogether different from our own: we would have to identify with the ancient world, up to the hour of its decline. The history of the Roman Empire is also a history of subversion, the history of an Empire of the Masses, the subversion of that Empire by the masses, who swallowed and annulled the ruling minorities and installed themselves in their place. The phenomenon of crowding and agglomeration likewise occurred. In consequence, as Oswald Spengler has so well observed, there arose a need to construct, then as now, enormous buildings.[1] The epoch of the masses is the epoch of the colossal.*

We live under the brutal reign of the masses. Precisely: we have now twice called this reign "brutal," we have now paid our tribute to the god of the commonplace. So that, voucher

---

* The tragedy inherent in this process is that, when the agglomeration developed, the depopulation of the countryside followed, bringing with it the absolute decrease in the total number of inhabitants within the Empire.

in hand, we can freely enter the theater, watch the spectacle
from inside. For did anyone think that this description of the
situation would be sufficient, exact as it may be? It is a description from outside, one face of the matter, one aspect of
the terrible phenomenon, as seen from the past alone. If I
were to drop the matter at this point, the reader could only
think, quite rightly, that the advent of the masses, a remarkable phenomenon, onto the world stage, onto the surface of
history, had inspired in me merely some disdainful words, a
measure of execration and a dash of repugnance, especially as
it is a matter of notoriety that I uphold a radically aristocratic
interpretation of history.* It is a *radical* view, inasmuch as I
have never held that human society *ought* to be aristocratic.
I have gone beyond that. I have held and continue to hold,
with a conviction that grows by the day, that human society
is aristocratic, always, whether it wants to be or not. And this
is true by reason of its very essence, to the point that it is truly
a society in the measure that it is aristocratic, and ceases to
be in the measure in which it ceases to be aristocratic. I am
speaking now of course, of society, not of the state. Surely,
no one can believe that, faced with the fantastic new world
teeming with masses, the proper aristocratic response is merely
to make some mannered gesture of disapprobation in the fashion of a fop at Versailles. For that place, the Versailles of
mannered gestures, was not aristocratic, but altogether the
contrary: it was the deathbed and the seat of dissolution and
putrefaction of a grand aristocracy. And the only truly aristocratic vestige left those people was the dignity they displayed

* See *España invertebrada*, 1921, date of its first publication as
a series of articles in the daily newspaper *El Sol*. (It is important to
point out to foreigners who generously comment on my books and
who frequently find it difficult to ascertain the date of first publication, that almost all my work has appeared in the convenient guise
of newspaper articles, and that much of it has taken long years to
venture into book form.)

on their visits to the guillotine and the grace with which they bared their necks. They accepted it as a tumor accepts the surgeon's knife. No, for anyone who has a sense of the real and profound mission of aristocracy, the spectacle of the masses animates him as a slab of virgin marble animates a sculptor. Social aristocracy in no way resembles that minuscule set who give themselves alone the integral name of society, calling themselves "society." These people live on exchanging invitations: on inviting or not inviting one another. Inasmuch as everyone has his mission and *raison d'être*, the elegant people or "smart set" have theirs somewhere in this vast world, but their role is minimal, subordinate, and not to be compared to the herculean task incumbent on true, authentic aristocrats. I would not be adverse to discussing the sense inherent in this world of elegance, so senseless on the face of it, but our theme is one of far greater dimensions. Of course, we find that this same "distinguished society" is attuned to the times. I was given food for thought by a young lady in full flower, bursting with vivacity and modernity, a star of the first magnitude in the firmament of "smart-set" Madrid, when she told me "I can't stand a dance to which less than eight hundred people have been invited." This statement made clear that the mass style has triumphed in every area of life and that it permeates even those final redoubts which seemed reserved for "the happy few."[2]

I reject any interpretation of our time which does not see the positive significance below the surface of the present-day reign of the masses, and equally reject any pious acceptance of the phenomenon devoid of any shudder of dread. Every destiny is dramatic — and profoundly tragic. Whosoever has not felt the peril of his times palpitating in his very hands has not penetrated to the vitals of destiny, but has merely fondled its morbid cheek. In our time, the element of terror in our destiny is the overwhelming, violent, moral rebellion of the masses, a phenomenon which is indomitable, ineluctable, and equivocal — like all destiny. Where is it leading us? Is the phenomenon an absolute evil or a possible good? There it is, colossal, straddling our times like a giant, a cosmic question mark. It is of uncertain form, with something of the guillotine about it, something of the gallows, as it strives to transform itself into a triumphal arch.

The phenomenon we must dissect possesses two dimensions. First, the masses today play a part in a repertory which formerly and exclusively belonged to select minorities. Second, and simultaneously, the masses have become intractable; they do not comply, they do not follow, they do not respect the natural minorities: they push them aside and supplant them.

Let us analyze the first dimension, in regard to which I would point out that the masses have assumed the benefits and pleasures, as well as the means for these advantages, which had been developed by the select minorities and which the latter had formerly enjoyed exclusively. Now, the masses have developed tastes, appetites, even "needs," of a type formerly classified as "refinements"—for in the past they were the patrimony of the few. Here is a trivial example: in the year 1820 there could not have been more than ten private bathrooms in all of Paris (as one can learn from the *Memoirs of the Comtesse de Boigne*).[3] Today, as a matter of course the masses make daily use of the means and technical accomplishments previously available only to select individuals.

And, not only do they have the advantage of material techniques, but more importantly, of social benefits and of the laws. In the eighteenth century, a minority group discovered that every human being, by right of birth alone, without need of any special qualification whatsoever, was possessed of certain fundamental political rights, the so-called rights of man and the citizen, and that these rights common to all are, strictly speaking, the only rights there are. Every other right, every right concerned with talent and natural endowments, was condemned as special privilege. At first, all this was pure theory, a mere theorem, the idea of a few. Later, however, these few were able to begin putting the idea into practice, and then, to impose it, and demand its acceptance — thus themselves becoming the "best" minority. Nevertheless, throughout the nineteenth century, the masses, enthusiastic as they might have become with the notion that these rights were a grand ideal, did not have any sense themselves of these ideas as such, did not exercise these rights, did not attempt to make them prevail; rather, they went on living, under democratic legislation, as before, as they had done under the *ancien regime*. The "people," as they then began to be called, learned that they were sovereign — but they did not believe it. Today that ideal has been converted into reality, not merely in the form of legislation, which is an external schema for public life, but in the heart of each individual, whatever his ideas, even if they be reactionary: that is to say, *even when the individual stomps on the very institutions which give those rights sanction.* In my opinion, whoever does not comprehend the curious moral position of the masses cannot possibly understand anything about what has begun to happen in the world today. The sovereignty of the unqualified individual, of the generic human being as such, has passed from being the juridical idea or ideal it had been in the past to being a psychological state already inbred in the average man. Now consider: whenever an ideal becomes a reality, it ceases to be an ideal; when it becomes a fundamental ingredient of reality, it ceases, inexorably, to be any part of an ideal. The natural magic of an ideal, the spell cast by it, evaporates. The leveling demands born out of ample democratic ideals have changed from being aspirations into being appetites and unconscious presumptions.

Now, the aim of these proclaimed rights was none other than to lift human souls from out of their inner servitude and to furnish them a conscious measure of self-mastery and self-dignity. Wasn't that the aim? Was it not desired that the average man should feel himself lord and master of himself and of his life? That has been accomplished. Why then the complaints from the liberals, the democrats, the progressives of yesteryear? Is it, perhaps, that like children, they want a certain something — but not its consequences? The aim was to make the common man a lord and master. Then why the surprise that he acts by and for himself, that he demands all the benefits, all the enjoyments, that he asserts his will, that he refuses any service, that he ceases to obey anyone, that he looks out for his own person and his own leisure, that he sees to his gear, to his clothes. These are all perennial attributes of being a lord and master. Today we find these qualities in the common man, in the mass.

We find, in short, that the life of the common man now encompasses the vital or living repertory which formerly characterized the minority at the top. Now then: the common man represents the ground over which any epoch's history moves. He is to history what sea-level is to geography.[4] If, then, the mean-level today reaches a height previously reached only by the aristocracies, it is patently clear that the level of history has suddenly risen — after long, subterranean preparation, of course, but obviously by a sudden leap, at a bound and in a generation. Human life, as a whole, has bounded upward. Today's soldier, for example, has something of the officer in him. He thinks himself a captain. The human army is now full of captains. We need only observe the energy, the determination, the free and easy style with which anybody at all moves through life, seizing any passing pleasure or fancy, and making his decision count.

Everything good and everything bad in the present and the immediate future has its root and cause in the general rise of the historic level. Here, an unpremeditated observation occurs to us. It is that while the ordinary level of life now, formerly reserved for a minority, is a novelty in Europe, it is not in America, where it is native and constitutional. To see my point clearly, let the reader but consider the matter of equality before the law, and the awareness of this fact in America. The psychological state attendant on feeling oneself lord and master of oneself and equal in law to any other individual, which in Europe only the eminent were able to achieve, has existed in America ever since the eighteenth century (thus, prevalent from the beginning: a constant from the start), a reality throughout American history. And another noteworthy fact, still more curious, is the following. When the present psychological state of the common man in Europe developed, when the level of his entire existence rose, the manner and tone of European life, among all orders, acquired a new face, a new physiognomy, one which caused many to say: "Europe is becoming Americanized." Those who spoke in this fashion gave the phenomenon no further importance; they believed it to be a matter of a slight change in custom, a mere fashion, and, deceived by external appearances, they attributed it to some influence or other of America on Europe. To my mind, that is an oversimplification of a question which is much more subtle, surprising, and deep-seated.

If I were magnanimous and gallant, I might here inform the Americans that they have succeeded in Americanizing Europe. But truth jousts with gallantry, and truth must prevail. Europe has not just been Americanized, not just like that. The process has begun, but it did not begin in the recent past, and flower in the present. We are faced with a dire accumulation of misconceptions, blinding both Americans and Europeans to the truth. The triumph of the masses and the enormous rise in the level of living has come about in Europe for internal reasons, after two centuries of mass-education in the concept of progress and a parallel socio-economic improvement. And it so happens that the result coincides with the most characteristic aspect of American life. Since the moral position of the common man in Europe coincides with that of the common man in America, the European, for the first time, comprehends American life, which was formerly an enigma and a total mystery to him. It is not a matter of influence, then, which would have been quite strange in itself—for it would have to have been not an in-fluence but a re-fluence—

instead it is something rather more unexpected, and that is, a simple leveling. The Europeans have always darkly observed that the average level of life was higher in America than in the older continent. This intuitive unanalytic certainty, obvious on the face of it, gave rise to the idea, never challenged, that the future lay with America. Clearly, such an ample idea, widespread and deep-rooted, was not borne on the wind, in the way that orchids are said to grow rootless in the air. The basis of the notion was the glimpse of the truth that the average level of life across the seas was higher than in Europe — along with the contrasting fact that life for the select minorities was lower. And history, like agriculture, gets its sustenance from the valleys and not from the heights, from the median social level and not from the prominence.

We live in a leveling era. Incomes are leveled, culture is leveled among the different social classes, and the sexes are leveled. Yes, and continents are also leveled. And though the vitality of the European continent was lower, it is now the gainer because of this economic leveling. In consequence, looked at from this point of view, the upheaval of the masses, brings with it a fabulous gain in living possibilities, the exact opposite of all we hear about the decadence of Europe. The decadence of Europe indeed![5] A misbegotten notion at best. It is a gauche phrase, in any case, which does not make clear whether we are speaking of European states, of European culture, or of what exists beneath it all and which is of far greater importance, namely, European vitality. Of European states and culture we shall have a word to say later on. But as regards Europe's vitality, it would be pertinent to mention that when dealing with its decline we are dealing with a gross error. Stated in another way, giving it a slight turn, my assertion may appear more convincing or at least less improbable. I assert, then, that today the average Italian, the average Spaniard, the average German is less different in vital tone from a Yankee or an Argentinian than he was a generation or two ago. And this is a basic fact that Americans should not forget.

3

The Level of the Times

THE REIGN OF THE MASSES does have one favorable aspect, inasmuch as it implies an overall rise in the entire historical level. It signifies that average existence today takes place on a higher level or altitude than it did in the past. This development brings home to us the fact that life can be lived at different levels at different times. Consequently, we can sensibly speak of the level of the times.[1] We can, in short, make good use of this expression, for it will reveal to us one of the most surprising characteristics of our epoch.

It is said, for example, that such and such is not in consonance with the level of the times. In effect, time always has a certain level, a certain elevation. We are speaking now of vital time, life time, what each generation calls "our time," and not of abstract chronological time which is all of one level, a temporal plain. Vital time, "our time," always presents a certain elevation: today looms over yesterday, or remains at the same level, or falls below it. The idea of falling implicit in the word "decadence" has its origin in this intuition. Moreover, every individual has a notion, more or less clear to him, of his own life's relationship with the level of the time in which he exists. Some will feel like castaways who cannot keep afloat amid the turbulence of their time, amid the modes and manners of the time given them. The fast tempo of modern life, the energetic pace and impetus, confound the man of archaic bent, and his anguish is a sign of the imbalance, the difference between his own level and that

of the times. On the other hand, whoever fully lives by present modes and manners will be aware of the relation between
our level and that of diverse times past. And what is this
relation?

It would be an error to think that a man of one era always
considers past eras—simply because they are past—to be inferior to his own.

To the poet Jorge Manrique it seemed that

> Any bygone time
> was better by far.[2]

But that judgment is not true either. Neither has every age
felt itself inferior to some past age, nor have all ages felt
superior to the past ages they can recall. Every historical age
manifests a different reaction toward the strange phenomenon of the "vital level," the level of life at the time. The importance of such attitudes and reactions makes it surprising
that thinkers and philosophers have not previously taken
them into account, for they are evident and substantially
important.

In general, Jorge Manrique's feeling has been the most
common reaction in past ages. And, in the majority of
epochs, people did not think their time was grander than
preceding epochs. Rather, the most usual attitude has been
for men to dream of better times in a vague past, of a more
fulfilling time, of a previous fuller existence; they have
spoken of a "Golden Age," as the Greek and Latin heritage
puts it; the Australian aborigines have their *Alcheringa*.[3] All
this shows us that those men felt that their own lives were
more or less lacking in plenitude, that their veins were not
filled to the full. And so they felt a respect for the past, for
"classic" times, when existence seemed to have been more
ample, richer, more perfect, more varied than their own. On
looking backward and imagining those worthier times, they
did not think themselves above those past times, but thought
rather that they were below them. It was as if a degree in

temperature — had it possessed any mite of consciousness — felt that it did not contain in itself a higher degree, but rather that any higher degree would necessarily contain more calories than it could probably contain itself. From A.D. 150 on, the feeling of shrinking vitality, of a decline and decay, of life's pulse slowing down, spread through the Roman Empire. Horace had already chanted his lines: "What do the ravages of time not injure! Our parents' age, worse than our grandsires', has brought us forth less worthy, and destined soon to yield an off-spring still more wicked."[4]

Two centuries later, there were not, in the whole Empire, enough men of Italic birth with sufficient fiber to serve as replacements for the centurions. It proved necessary to hire men for this rank from among the Dalmatians, and later, from among the barbarians of the Danube and the Rhine. Meanwhile, women were growing increasingly sterile, and Italy became depopulated.

Let us look now at other kinds of eras, those which possess a vital quality quite contrary to the last mentioned. Here we are faced with a most curious phenomenon, one highly important to define. At the beginning of the twentieth century, opposition politicians addressing their audiences were in the habit of condemning a government edict or blunder as being "out of keeping with the full measure of the times." Strange to recall that this was the kind of phrase used by Trajan in his famous letter to Pliny, where he recommended that Christians should not be persecuted on the basis of anonymous accusations for it would not be "in keeping with the spirit of our times."[5] There have been, then, various epochs in history which have felt themselves to have achieved a full, definitive high point, a time in which they have arrived at the end of a journey, a time in which an age-old goal has been attained, a hope completely fulfilled. Thus, "the full measure of the times" = the complete maturity of historic life. At the beginning of the twentieth century, in effect, the European believed that human life had become what it was meant to be, what generations had wished it to be, what it was henceforward always bound to be. These epochs of plenitude always regard themselves as the end-result of many other ages, all preparatory; as the sum of ages without plenitude, ages inferior to their own present, ages on top of which their time has bloomed in full flower. Seen from their own "height," previous preparatory ages appear to have been times when life was a matter of pure longing and unsatisfied desire, of illusions only, of eager precursors, of "Not yet!," and of a painful contrast between a clear aspiration and an uncorresponding reality. Thus did the nineteenth century look upon the Middle Ages, thus did it consider that time to have been. At last the day dawns on which that ancient, age-long desire seems to have been attained: reality recognizes the signs, and accepts its good fortune. We have reached the heights, the heights we had seen in the distance, the goal we had foreseen, the summit of time. "Not yet!" has given way to "At last!"

That was the view our progenitors held in the nineteenth century. Let us not forget that our epoch is one which follows an epoch which felt itself to be one of plenitude. So that from the other shore in time, a man from out of the past would look upon us with an optical illusion: we would strike him as decadent.

But a devotee of history,[6] a man who has taken the pulse of many an epoch, cannot be deceived by optical illusions or by feelings of so-called plenitude.

According to our definition, "a period of plenitude" occurs only at the end of a centuries-old longing, when the goal seems to have been achieved. And so it is: times of plenitude are times of self-satisfaction. Sometimes, as in the nineteenth century, epochs are more than satisfied with themselves.* By

---

* The inscriptions on the face of Hadrian's coinage carry such phrases / messages as *Italia Felix* and *Saeculum aureum* and *Tellus stabilita* and *Temporum felicitas*. It is useful to consult Cohen's

now, we know that these centuries of such satisfaction, so full of achievement, were dead on the inside. *Authentic integrity, vital fullness, do not consist in self-satisfaction, in achievement, in final arrival.* As Cervantes wrote long ago: "The road is always better than the inn." Any epoch that has satisfied its ideal desires is one which no longer feels desire, one whose wells and founts of desire have run dry. In short, our vaunted plenitude is, in reality, a conclusion. There are centuries which, from an impotence and an inability to rekindle their desire, die of self-satisfaction, just as the happy drone dies after his nuptial flight.*

And hence, the surprising fact that these epochs of so-called plenitude have always, in the depths of their consciousness, felt a most peculiar sadness.

The age-old desire so long in gestation which seemed at last to have come to realization in the nineteenth century is that which called itself "modern culture." The very name is alarming: that a century should call itself "modern," that is, ultimate, definitive, compared to which all others are merely preterite, humble preparations aspiring to the present! Pointless arrows which missed the mark!†

---

great work on numismatics, and also the coins reproduced in Rostovtzeff's *Social and Economic History of the Roman Empire*, 1926, plate Lii, and p. 588, note 6.

[Mishael Ivanovic Rostovtzeff (1870-1952), Russian-American historian, also wrote *A History of the Ancient World* (1926-27).]

  * Only read the wonderful pages by Hegel in his *Philosophy of History*.

  † The original meaning of 'modern', 'modernity', words with which recent times have christened themselves, demonstrates quite clearly the feeling of being up to the 'level of the times,' the very concept being analyzed here. Modern is whatever is in accordance with the *mode, à la mode*, 'in fashion': the new mode is meant, of course, a mode or modification, a fashion which has come about

Does one not sense here an essential difference between our time and the times just passed? Our time, in point of fact, no longer feels itself to be definitive. On the contrary, it radically discovers, obscurely intuits that there are no such definitive times, no epochs crystalized forever; quite the opposite, the presumption that a certain way of life, even so-called "modern culture," should be definitive, seems an obfuscation, a narrowing of sight, a near-blindness in the field of vision. Once we realize this, we can enjoy the sensation of having escaped from a hermetically sealed enclosure, of having regained freedom and of having emerged again into the open, to stand under the stars in the real world, the deep, endless, inexhaustible, authentic, terrifying world without limits, where everything is possible, the best and the worst.

Such faith in modern culture was a melancholy one: it meant that tomorrow would be in every essential the same as today, that progress consisted in advancing from one *always* to another *always* along a road identical to the one under one's feet. A road like that is more like a prison which stretches out, elastically, without any vista of freedom.

In the early days of the Roman Empire, when a cultured provincial came to Rome—someone like Lucan, say, or Seneca —and for the first time saw the majestic Imperial buildings, symbols of a definitive enduring power, his heart would contract. Surely nothing new could now occur in the world. Rome was eternal. And if there is a melancholy surrounding ancient ruins, a melancholy which rises from them like mist from a neap-tide, there was a melancholy no less perceptible to any sensitive provincial, even if for opposite reasons: the

---

at that present moment as against the old traditional modes of the past. The word 'modern' expresses, then, consciousness of new life, superior to the old, antique life, and at the same time, it is an imperative call to rise to the level of the times, to the height of its style. In the eyes of a 'modern' man, not to be modern is to fall below the level of history.

melancholy of buildings meant for eternity.

Over against this state of mind, our feelings in this age are more boisterous. Do we not act like noisy children in joyous hubbub on being let out of school? Today we no longer know what will happen in the world of tomorrow, and that secretly pleases us. For that very unpredictability, the impossibility of knowing what is ahead, the fact that our horizon is open to all possibilities, constitutes the true fullness, the plenitude of life, of authentic life.

This diagnosis — which is only half the story, to be sure, the other half yet to be told — is in contrast to the plaints about decadence found in the tearful pages of so much early twentieth century writing. We are dealing here with an optical illusion, an error of vision stemming from a number of causes. We shall examine some of them, but for the moment let us consider the most obvious, which is that certain writers, bound by an ideology which seems to me superseded, look at history only in its political and cultural aspects and fail to note that these aspects are merely the surface of history, that the reality of history is, most deeply, a pure lust for life, pure vitality, a power in man similar to cosmic energy,[7] not the same as, not identical with, but related to the energy which agitates the sea, fecundates the beasts, drives the trees to bloom and the stars to shine.

Confronted with the diagnoses of decadence, I advance the following consideration:

Decadence is, of course, a comparative concept. Decline takes place from a higher to a lower state. But the comparison may be made from the most varied points of view imaginable. To the manufacturer of amber cigar-holders this is a decadent world, for nowadays scarcely anyone smokes through amber mouthpieces. Other viewpoints may be more substantial than this one, and yet none of them escapes being partial, arbitrary, external to life itself, and it is life's value we are attempting to assay. There is only one justifiable and altogether natural point of view, and that one proceeds from within life itself. It develops when one takes one's stance inside life and reflects on it from within, ascertaining whether or not it, life, senses that it is decadent, that it is diminished, debilitated, spiritless.

Even when we consider life from "within," how can we know if it feels itself to be in decline or not? There is one decisive symptom: a life which does not prefer any other past form, any other past at all, and which therefore prefers itself, can in nowise be called decadent. And here we have the point to which all the discussion about the level of the times was leading. For it so happens that precisely our own time enjoys a new and rare sensation, a strange sensation — unique, as far as I know, in recorded history.

In the literary salons of the last century, there was always sure to be a moment when the cultured ladies and their domesticated poets would play the game of asking each other "In which age would you have chosen to live?" And they all would start off straight-away, their personal packs on their backs, to wander in imagination through the highways and byways of history in search of a time in which they might most happily pitch their tents. What this demonstrates is that although the nineteenth century felt it was itself a time of plenitude, it was in fact still linked to the past, upon whose shoulders it was thought to be standing: it saw itself as the culmination of the past. It believed in more or less classic ages — the century of Pericles, the Renaissance — during which times its own current values had been prepared and formed. This fact in itself should be enough to make us cautiously examine times of so-called plenitude. Their gaze was turned backward, they looked to a past now being fulfilled in themselves.

Well then, what would be the honest reply of any representative man of the present to such a question as the one posed above? There is not much doubt about it, I would think: any past time, without exception, would strike him as being a restricted space, a narrow redoubt wherein he could not breathe. In short, the man of the present believes that his own life is more of a life than all former lives in the past, or inversely, that present day humanity has outgrown all of the past put together. The elementary clarity of this intuition about our life today annuls any and all lucubrations concerning decadence, unless they be cautionary only.

To begin with, then, life today feels itself more ample, larger in scope, than all previous lives. How could it feel decadent? Quite the contrary is true. Through sheer self-regard for its fuller life, it has lost all respect, all consideration for the past. Hence, we have, for the first time, an epoch which makes a *tabula rasa* of all classicism, which finds nothing in the past to serve as a possible model or norm. And thus the present — which is the culmination of so many centuries of evolutionary continuity — gives the impression of a mere beginning, a new dawning, an initiation, an infancy. We look back, and the famous Renaissance strikes us as a narrow provincial time, full of vapid gestures and — why not say so? — *kitsch*: vulgar and pretentious.

My own summary of the situation appeared some time ago: "The acute disassociation between past and present is the sign of our times, a generic factor of the epoch, and with it arises a suspicion, more or less vague, which engenders the restlessness peculiar to life in our times. Present-day man feels alone on the face of the earth, and suspects that the dead did not die 'in jest but in earnest,' not ritually but factually, and can no longer help us. The remnants of the traditional spirit have evaporated. Norms, models, standards are of no further use. We must resolve our problems without the active collaboration of the past, totally confined to the present — whether our problems be in art, science, or politics. Modern man finds himself alone, without any living ghosts at his side. Like Peter Schlemiel he has lost his shadow. That is what always happens at high noon."*

* *La deshumanizacion del arte.*

What is, in short, the "level of our times"?

It is not a time of plenitude, and yet, it is a time which feels itself superior to all known times and above all known plenitudes. It is not easy to formulate the opinion this epoch has of itself: it believes it is superior to all others and, at the same time, it feels that it is a new beginning—and yet wonders if it is not in its death-throes. How shall we put it? Perhaps this way: this time is more than past times, and less than itself. Powerful, and uncertain of its destiny. Proud of its strength and fearful of its might.

4

The Increase in Life

THE REIGN OF THE MASSES, the rise in the level of life, and the consequent increased level of the times are all symptoms of a more general and complex phenomenon. The latter is quite incredible on the face of it: the world in this century has grown, and with it and in it so has life itself, for life has become universalized. The world of the average man today is the universe. The individual "lives" the entire world. Even in the earlier part of the century, I remember the way the whole city of Seville followed, hour by hour, through the popular press, what was happening to a few men at the Pole: it was as though icebergs drifted across the burning plains of Andalusia. And now any given piece of earth is no longer restricted merely to its geographic, geometric position but is, for many purposes, affecting other portions of the planet. According to the law of physics which holds that things are wherever their effects are felt, any point in the world is today effectively ubiquitous. This proximity of the far-away, the presence of the absent, has vastly extended the horizon of every single life.

The world has grown in time. Archeology and prehistory have turned up time periods of amazing duration or extension, of near-chimerical proportions. Whole civilizations and empires whose very names were not even suspected a short time ago have been annexed to our memories like new continents. Photo-journalism and the screen have brought the remotest portions of the globe into the immediate field of everyone's vision.

Everything else being equal, the spatio-temporal expansion of the world would not in itself signify anything. For in themselves physical space and time represent absolute absurdity in the world.[1] Hence there is more reason than is generally assumed in the worship of pure speed, speed in itself, transitorily indulged in by our contemporaries. Speed, made up of space and time, is no less absurd than its component parts. But it serves to annul them. One absurdity cannot be nullified except by another. For man it is a question of honor to triumph over cosmic space and time*—which are completely devoid of any sense—and it is not surprising that we derive a puerile pleasure from manipulating empty speed, by means of which we assassinate space and annihilate time. By annulling them we lend them new life, we make them serve vital purposes: we can *be* in more places than ever before, take pleasure in more comings and goings, consume in less life-time more cosmic-time.

In the final analysis, however, the substantive expansion of our world is not a matter of larger dimensions, but the fact that it contains more *things*. Each of these things—let us take the word in its most comprehensive sense—is "some-thing" we can desire, attempt, do, undo, find, enjoy—even reject— and all of these verbs imply vital action.

Take any one of our activities: buying, for example. Let us imagine two men, one from the present and one from the eighteenth century, each of equal fortune, in relative proportion to the value of money in the periods, and compare the stock of goods offered to each of the two. The difference is well-nigh fabulous. The quantity of possibilities available to present-day buyers is practically limitless. It is hard to imagine or want something not already on the market and, con-

---

* Precisely because man's lifetime is limited, precisely because he is mortal, he must overcome distance and slowness. The automobile would have no meaning at all for an immortal God.

versely, it is not easy to imagine and want everything already on sale. The objection might be made that, with a relatively equal fortune, a person today cannot buy more things than a man of the eighteenth century. This is not the case. Much more can be bought today, because industry has cheapened the cost of almost everything. But even if the objection were true, it would only strengthen my point.

The activity of buying comes to an end with the decision to buy a certain object; but it is first of all a matter of selecting, and selection begins with a consideration of the possibilities offered by the market. Hence it follows that life, in the area of purchasing, consists in rehearsing the buying possibilities as such. In speaking of life, one of the fundamental essentials is often forgotten: at every turn and before all else our lives are a conscious awareness of what is possible, possible for us. If we had only one possibility before us at a given moment, it would be meaningless to call it a "possibility." It would be a matter of utter necessity. But here we encounter the strangest of facts, namely that a fundamental condition of our existence is always to find ourselves confronted with a variety of prospects. And because they are various, they become possibilities among which we must make a choice.* To say that we live is to say we find ourselves surrounded by certain determined possibilities. These surroundings are said to be our "circumstances."† All life is a matter of finding oneself in one's "circumstance," or one's world. For this is the original meaning of the idea "world." The world is the sum-

* In the worst of cases, when the world seems to offer only one way out, there are always two: either the one proffered, or the way out of the world. But to quit the world is part of the world, just as a door is part of a room.

† This notion already appears in the prologue of my first book, *Meditaciones del Quijote* (1916). In *Las Atlántidas* it appears under the name of "horizon." See the essay "El origen deportivo del Estado" (1962) in vol. VII of *El Espectador*.

total of our vital, or life, possibilities. It is not something apart from or alien to our life, but rather its true periphery. It represents what each of us can be, our vital potential, our potentiality. In order to be realized, it must be lived to a conclusion. In fact, we realize only a minimal part of what we might be. And thus the world seems enormous, and we, within it, a very small matter. The world, the possibilities of our life, is always much greater than our destiny or our actual life.

The only point to make here, however, is that the life of man has grown in the dimension of its potentiality. He can nowadays count on a range of possibilities far greater than ever before. In the intellectual sphere he can find more avenues of possible speculation, more problems, more data, more science, more possible points of view. Where the number of occupations or careers in primitive life could be counted almost on the fingers of one hand (shepherd, hunter, warrior, soothsayer) the number today is nearly endless, superlatively extended. The range of pleasures is similarly varied, although (and this is a phenomenon more serious than is commonly assumed) the catalogue of pleasures is not as extraordinary as those of other aspects of life. Nevertheless, for the average man in the cities — and cities are the representative locations of modern existence — the possibilities of enjoyment have increased fantastically in this century.

Still the growth in vital potential is not limited to what has been said thus far. It has also increased in ways that are more immediate and mysterious. It is a well-known and celebrated fact that performances in physical sport today set records greatly surpassing all past performances. It is not a matter of admiring each individual feat, but of noting the frequency with which records fall, so that we are left with the impression that the human organism today possesses far greater capacity than ever before. A similar phenomenon is developing in science, where in only a few decades its cosmic horizon has widened incredibly. Einstein's physics moves through spaces so vast that the antique physics of Newton occupies only attic-space within it.* And this extensive increase is due to an intensive increase in scientific precision. Einsteinean physics came about through close attention to minimal differences previously disregarded as being of no importance in sum. The atom, located at the boundaries of the world of yesteryear, is today so amplified as to be in itself an entire planetary system. And we mention all this without reference to what it might mean for the perfection of culture—not at issue here—but merely to note the growth of the subjective potential this development implies. There is no need to stress the fact that Einsteinean physics may be more exact than the Newtonian equivalent, but we merely note that Einstein the man is capable of greater exactitude and is freer of spirit† than the man Newton, just as a champion boxer today is able to deliver more formidable blows than fighters ever did before.

Just as film and the illustrated press bring the remotest areas of the planet before the eyes of the average man, so do newspapers and informed comment bring news of remote intellectual *performances*. Shop windows and storefronts offer convincing displays of the latest inventions. Thus does the average man get an impression of fabulous potential all around him.

I do not mean to say that life is better today than in other

---

* Newton's world was infinite, but this infinity was not a matter of size, but an empty generalization, an abstract and vain utopia. Einstein's world is finite, but concrete and full in every part, and therefore a world richer in things and, effectively, larger in size.

† Freedom of spirit, that is, intellectual potential, is measured by the ability to dissociate ideas traditionally inseparable. To dissociate is more difficult than to associate, as [Wolfgang] Kohler has demonstrated in his investigations on the intelligence of chimpanzees. Never before has human understanding possessed greater capacity to dissociate than now.

times. It is not the quality of life today that we have been discussing, but only its growth, is quantitative advance and increase in potential. The discussion involves a description of modern man's consciousness, of his vital tone, which consists in his feeling himself equipped with a greater potential than ever before, so that to him the past seems dwarfed.

The purpose here is to counter the lucubrations over decadence, especially over the Decline of the West, which have filled the air since the 1920s. The points made above are as obvious as they are simple. There is no purpose in speaking of decadence unless it is made clear what is in decline. Does this pessimistic term refer to culture? Is there, then, a decadence in European culture? Or is there rather simply a decadence in European national organizations? Let us assume the latter to be the case. Is that cause enough to speak of Western decadence? By no means. Partial decadence is a matter of decline related only to secondary elements in history — to culture and nations. And there is only one absolute decadence: it consists of a declining vitality, and it exists only when it is felt. And that is why I have taken the time to consider a phenomenon which is often overlooked: the conscious awareness that each epoch has of its own level of vitality.

The initial discussion led us to speak of the "plenitude" some centuries have sensed as against other centuries which, in turn, saw themselves as being in decline from greater heights, from ancient brilliant golden ages. And I concluded by noting the quite obvious fact that our age is characterized by the strange presumption that it is "more" than any past age. Furthermore: our age ignores the entire past and refuses to recognize classic, normative epochs, but sees itself as representative of a new life superior to all ancient forms of life and looks upon itself as unconnected with any simpler state in the past.

I doubt if our era can be understood without serious consideration of these observations. For here we have precisely the problem of the time. If it felt it was decadent, declining, then it would look upon other epochs as superior to itself, and that would mean it admired them, esteemed them, and venerated the principles by which they were inspired. Our time would then have clear and firmly held ideals, even if it were incapable of realizing them. The truth is quite the contrary: we live at a time which feels itself magnificently capable of any realization, but does not know what to realize. Lord of all things, man is not master of himself. He feels lost in his own abundance. Equipped with more means, more knowledge, more technique than ever, the world today proceeds as did the worst and most unfortunate of all former worlds: it simply drifts.

Hence the strange duality—a sense of vast potential and a sense of insecurity dwelling side by side in the spirit of modern man. He is in the same position as Louis XV's Regent, who was said to have had all the talents, except the talent to use them. To the nineteenth century, firm though it was in its faith in progress, many things seemed *already* impossible. Today, since everything seems possible, we sense that the worst is also possible: retrogression, barbarism, decadence.* This itself would not be a bad symptom. It would indicate that we had again made contact and were in concert with the essential insecurity of all life, with the restlessness, painful but also delightful, that comes from living each moment to its core, to its raw and palpitating vitals. Ordinarily we avoid feeling that fearsome pulse which gives each moment of truth a life of its own. In striving to find security, we render ourselves insensible to the bare drama of our destiny, burying it in the habitual, the ready-made, and the topical—all of which finally anesthetize us. It is just as well, then, even beneficial, that for the first time in almost three centuries we are suddenly, surprisingly confronted with the feeling that

* Herein is the root-origin of decadence: not that we *are* decadent, but that, admitting all possibilities, we do not exclude the possibility of decadence.

we do not know what is going to happen tomorrow.

Anyone who seriously confronts his own existence, and makes himself fully responsible for it, is bound to feel a certain unease which will put him on guard.[2] The orders of the Roman Army to a sentry of the Legion specified that he keep his index finger on his lips to avoid drowsiness and to keep him on the alert. Not a bad gesture, for it seems to impose a greater silence on the surrounding night's silence, to enable one to hear the secret germination of the future. The security of epochs of "plenitude" — such as the nineteenth century — is an optical illusion which leads to neglect of the future, all direction of which is handed over to the mechanism of the universe. Both progressive liberalism and Marxist socialism presume that what is desired by them as the best of all possible futures will be inexorably realized with a necessity like that of astronomy. Their consciousness lulled by this idea, these "progressivists" have let go the helm of history, ceased to keep watch, and have lost their footing. So, life has slipped from their grasp; it has proven unsubmissive and wanders off on its own, on no known course. Beneath the mask of a generous futurism, the progressivist does not really preoccupy himself with the future, for he is convinced that it holds few secrets or surprises, no profound reversals or essential innovations. Assured that the world will now proceed on a straight course, without detours or deviations, the progressivist allays any unease about the future and installs himself in the definitive present, the all-encompassing present where he takes his stand. It is not surprising that the world seems emptied of purpose, anticipation, and authentic ideals. Few are concerned with supplying them. Such has been the desertion, the treason of the minorities, of the minorities who are supposed to direct! Here we have the other side of the coin in the rebellion of the masses. But let us return to a consideration of this rebellion. After having examined the favorable side of the triumph of the masses, it would be only right to let ourselves down the other slope, the more dangerous one.

5

A Statistical Fact

THIS ESSAY is an attempt to suggest a diagnosis for our time, a diagnosis of present-day existence. The first point is clearly stated: life today, considered as a repertory of possibilities, is magnificent, superior to all others known to history. But precisely because its format is larger, it has managed to overflow all known channels: its scope is so great that it has swept away all the principles and ideals handed down by tradition. It has more life than all past life, and consequently it is more problematic. It cannot orient itself in the past.* It must invent its own destiny.

Life, which means primarily what it is possible for us to be, possible life, is similarly a matter of making a choice, from among the possibilities, of what we actually are going to be. Circumstance and decision, our circumstances and our decisions, are the two root-elements of life. Circumstance — that is, the possibilities — is the part given us, imposed on us. These possibilities constitute what we call our world. Life does not choose its own world, and to live is to find oneself in a world already determined and unchangeable: the world of the present. Our world is the portion of destiny which makes up our life. But this vital destiny, or life-destiny, is not

---

* We shall see, nevertheless, how it is possible to obtain from the past, if not positive orientation, much negative counsel. The past can scarcely tell us what we ought to do, but it can tell us what we ought to avoid.

a mechanical destiny. We are not fired at existence like a bullet from a rifle, for a bullet has a trajectory which is absolutely predetermined. The destiny we fall into, when we fall into this world—and the world is always *this* world *now*—is the opposite of a rifle-barrel. Instead of imposing a single trajectory upon us, it imposes several and, consequently, forces us to choose. A surprising condition, that of our existence! To live is to feel *fatally* forced to exercise liberty, to decide what we are going to be in this world. Not for an instant is our decision-making allowed to lapse. Even when in despair we abandon ourselves to whatever happens, we have made the decision not to decide.

It is false to say, therefore, that in life "circumstances decide." On the contrary: the circumstances are the dilemma, always new, constantly renewed, in the face of which we must make decisions. And it is our character which decides.

All the above holds equally true for the collective life, in which there is also, first, a horizon of possibilities, and then, a resolution which chooses and decides the effective form of the collective existence. This resolution emanates from the character of society, or what comes to the same, of the type of men dominant in it. In our time, the mass-man dominates, and it is he who decides. It is not correct simply to say that this began to happen with the advent of democracy, of mass-suffrage. The masses do not decide under universal suffrage; their role has consisted in adhering to one or another minority. The minorities presented their "programs"—an excellent word for the purpose. The programs were, in effect, programs for collective life. In them the mass was invited to accept a project for decision.

What happens today is quite different. If one observes the public life of the countries where the triumph of the masses has gone farthest (the Mediterranean countries among them), it it surprising to see how these countries live, politically, day by day. The phenomenon is extraordinary. Public authority is in the hands of mass-representatives. The masses are powerful enough to have wiped out all possible opposition. They are in possession of power in such an incontrovertible manner that it would be difficult to find in history any governments so unassailable. And yet, the public authority, the government, lives day to day. It does not represent any clear future, it does not stand for a visible tomorrow, it does not appear as the beginning of any credible or conceivable development. In short, it exists without any project for existence. It does not know where it is going because, strictly speaking, it merely goes, without any predetermined course or trajectory. When power seeks to justify itself, it does not mention the future, but rather it takes refuge in the present and seems to say, with some sincerity, "I am an abnormal government, made necessary by the circumstances." That is, by the urgency of the present moment, not by calculation for the future. Its acts are merely a matter of dodging the hourly conflicts, not of resolving them, but of avoiding them for the time being, using makeshift means and whatever comes along, at the cost of accumulating even greater conflicts for the next eventuality. Such has public power ever been when exercised directly by the masses: omnipotent and ephemeral. The mass-man is one whose life lacks purpose as he goes drifting along. Thus, he does not build anything substantial, though his possibilities and his powers are enormous.

And this is the type of man who makes the decisions in our time. It would be well to analyze his character.

The key to this analysis lies in the question we asked at the beginning of this work: Whence have come the multitudes which crowd the stage of history?

Some years ago, the eminent economist Werner Sombart[1] first laid emphasis on a most simple fact, which should be in the minds of all students of contemporary events. This simple fact should be enough to clear our vision of modern Europe, and if it is not enough, it should suffice in any case to put us on the right track. These are the facts: from the beginnings of European history in the sixth century to the year 1800 —

that is, through the course of twelve centuries—the population of Europe never exceeded 180 million. Then: from 1800
to 1914—that is, in little over a century—the population of
Europe increased from 180 million to 460 million! These
figures leave no doubt, I presume, as to the talent for proliferation shown in one century. In three generations a human
mass on a gigantic scale was produced, to the point that this
mass overflowed like a torrent onto the stage of history and
inundated it. This fact alone shows how the mass came upon
us and triumphed, and what the implications are. And that
is the most concrete sum in the equation of the rising level
of life, as we have already indicated.

The above data should serve, at the same time, to put
in perspective our somewhat unfounded amazement at the
growth of new nations such as the United States of America.
We marvel at its increasing size, which in one century was
boosted to 100 million, when the real marvel has been the
teeming fertility of Europe. And this is another reason to correct our illusion about the Americanization of Europe. Not
even the characteristic which might seem most specifically
American—the rapidity of increase in population—is pecu-
liarly its own. In that one century, Europe increased much
more than America did. And America was formed by the
overflow from Europe.

Though Werner Sombart's point is not as well known as it
should be, there is no need for an unnecessary insistence on
it, since a confused impression of the considerable increase of
European population has been widespread. It is not the simple increase of population shown by the figures that is of interest but the more basic fact they make clear: the vertiginous
rate of growth. That is of greater significance. That is the important point in this discussion. For this vertiginous rate of
increase means that heaps and heaps of people have been
thrust upon history pell-mell, at such an accelerated speed,
that it has been well-nigh impossible to incorporate them
into the traditional culture.

In effect, the average European is of a stronger and sounder fiber than in the previous century, but he is far more simple-minded. Thus it is that he often gives the impression of a primitive man suddenly and unexpectedly cast upon a very old civilization. In those same schools which were such a source of pride to the last century we can now do little more than instruct the masses in the techniques of modern living. It has not been possible to educate them. They have been given the tools for an intense form of living, but they have not been given any feeling or sensibility for the great historic tasks. They have been thoughtlessly inoculated with pride and power in modern means, but left unendowed with a corresponding spirit. Thus, they care nothing about spiritual values, these newer generations, as they propose to take command of the world as if it were a paradise without any trace of the past, without the complex traditional problems.

To the last century, then, falls the glory and responsibility of having let these multitudes loose on history. This fact gives us the most adequate perspective from which to judge that century fairly. There must have been something extraordinary about it when such rich harvests of human fruit were produced in its climate. Any deference shown principles which inspired former ages is both frivolous and ridiculous unless it gives clear signs of having comprehended these past marvels. All history seems to have been a gigantic laboratory where every experiment has been carried out in order to obtain a formula for public life favoring the plant "man." And, beyond all sophisticated reasoning, we find that the experiment of submitting human seed to the two conditions called liberal democracy and technology has led the European species to threefold growth, to tripling itself in a single century.

Such exuberant luxuriousness must force us, unless we prefer to be mindless, to draw some conclusions: first, that liberal democracy based on technical creativity is the highest form of public life so far known; second, that this form may not be the best imaginable, but that the best we can imagine must conserve the essence of these two principles: third, that to return to forms of life inferior to those of the nineteenth century would mean suicide.

Once we recognize all this with the clarity demanded by the facts, we are free to deal severely with the nineteenth century. If it is true that there was something incomparable about it, it is also true that it nurtured certain radical vices, certain constitutional defects, when it engendered a caste of men, mass-man in revolt, who place in immanent jeopardy the very principles to which they owe their existence. If that type of human continues to be master of Europe and to be the one definitively making the decisions, a few generations will suffice to take the continent back to barbarism. Industrial technology would break down, and legal processes would evanesce, in the same manner as technical secrets have often disappeared.* All of life would contract. The present abundance of possibilities would turn to a scarcity of them, to a shortage and to anguished impotence, to true decadence. For the rebellion of the masses is one and the same as what Rathenau called "the vertical invasion of the barbarians."[2]

It is of great importance, then, to closely examine this mass-man with his awesome potential for the greatest good and the greatest evil.

---

* Hermann Weyl, one of the greatest of physicists, Einstein's companion and continuator, was given to repeating, in private conversation, that if a certain ten or twelve individuals were to die suddenly, the marvel of present-day physics would die with them and almost certainly be forever lost to humanity. Many centuries of preparation had been necessary to adapt the mental organ to the abstract complexity of physical theory. Any chance event could annihilate such a prodigious human possibility, which is also the basis of future technical development.

[Hermann Weyl (1885-1955), German mathematican, who provided a link between pure mathematics and theoretical physics, and who added to quantum mechanics and to the theory of relativity.]

6

The Mass-Man Dissected

WHAT IS HE LIKE, this mass-man who today dominates public life, political and nonpolitical? Why is he as he is, and how has he come into being?

It would be best to answer these questions jointly, for they lend themselves to mutual clarification. The man who now aspires to leadership in public life is quite different from the men who led in the nineteenth century, though that century produced and prepared the new man for his current role. Any perceptive mind could have predicted, in 1820 or 1850 or 1880, by a simple act of a priori reasoning, the grave situation in which we find ourselves. In fact, nothing is happening which was not foreseen a hundred years ago. "The masses advance!" Hegel cried apocalyptically. Auguste Comte made the pronouncement: "Without a new spiritual force, our epoch, which is revolutionary, will end in catastrophe." And from a rock top in the Engadine the mustachioed Nietzsche cried out: "I see a flood-tide of nihilism rising." It is false to say that history cannot be foretold. It has been prophesied repeatedly. If the future offered no ground for prophecy, it could not be understood later when it came to pass nor after it had passed. The entire philosophy of history is summed up in the idea that the historian is a prophet in reverse. True, only the general structure of the future can be anticipated, but that is all we can truly understand of the past, or of the present for that matter. Accordingly, if one wants the best view of one's epoch, one must step back and look at it from a distance. At what distance? Very simple: the necessary distance to avoid seeing Cleopatra's nose.

What is life like for the "multitudinous man" the nineteenth century kept producing in ever-increasing numbers? To begin with, there is the ubiquitous appearance of every kind of material ease. Never before could the average man resolve his economic problems with greater facility. While the great fortunes proportionally declined and the existence of the industrial worker became more difficult, the average man of the middle classes found his economic horizon wider ever day. Every day he could add a new bounty to his living standard. Every day his position was more secure and less dependent on another's will. What before would have been considered a gift of good fortune, inspiring humble gratitude towards benevolent fate, became converted into a right, meriting no gratitude, but something to be demanded. Beginning about 1900, the worker also began to extend and ensure his existence. He had to struggle, nevertheless, to gain his end. Unlike the middle class man, he did not find benefits attentively served up to him by a society and a state that were wonders of organization.

To this economic facility and security must be added certain physical benefits: comfort and public order. His life must run as if on rails. Unexpected violence and danger must be kept at bay.

Such an open and bountiful existence was bound to instill in his deepest consciousness the notion that, as the acute and graceful folk-saying of our ancient country puts it, "Ample is Castile." That is to say, in all its elemental and decisive aspects, life presented itself to the new man as *exempt from restrictions*. The importance of this fact follows automatically when it is remembered that this sense of vital bounty was totally unavailable to the common man in the past. On the contrary, for him life was destined to be restricted, economically and physically. From birth, living meant an accumulation of burdens which he must bear, with no solution but to adapt and make do in the narrowest circumstances.

Even more evident is the contrast in situations if we pass from the material to the civil and moral plane. Beginning in the second half of the nineteenth century, the average man no longer finds social barriers raised against him. That is, he is no longer confronted from birth with obstacles and limitations in public life. No one can oblige him to put limits to his existence. Here again: "Ample is Castile." "Estates" and "castes" no longer exist. No one is civilly privileged. The average man learns that all men are legally equal.

Never in the course of history had man found himself in life-surroundings even remotely like those established in this new way. It is a radical innovation in human destiny, one gestated by the nineteenth century. A new stage has been constructed on which man may enact his existence, new in the physical and social sense. Three principles have made this new world possible: liberal democracy, scientific experimentation, and industrialization. The last two can be summed up in one word: technology. None of these principles was invented by the nineteenth century; they are the product of the two previous centuries. The glory of the nineteenth century, as everyone knows, comes not from the invention of these principles but from their implementation. But it is not enough to recognize this fact abstractly; we must understand the inevitable consequences.

The nineteenth century was in essence revolutionary. This essence is not to be sought on the barricades which in themselves do not constitute a revolution, but in the fact that this century established the average man — the great social mass — in conditions radically opposite to those which had always surrounded him. Public life was turned inside out. Revolution is not an uprising against an existing order, but the establishment of a new order reversing traditional order. Hence it is not an exaggeration to say that the man engendered by the nineteenth century is a man apart from all other men as regards matters of public life. Eighteenth-century man differs, of course, from the man dominant in the seventeenth century, and the latter from the sixteenth-century man, but they are all related, similar, even identical in essentials if they are compared to this new man. For the populace, the *vulgus*, of all epochs, "life" had meant, first of all, limitation, obligation, dependence: in a word, pressure. Call it oppression, if you like, as long as oppression be understood to be cosmic, as well as legal and social. For cosmic oppression was never absent from the world until the expansion of modern science —physical and administrative—to a practically limitless extent. Previously, even for the rich and powerful, the world was a place of poverty, difficulty, and danger.*

The world which surrounds the new man from the day of his birth scarcely impels him to limit himself in any fashion; it offers neither argument nor veto; on the contrary, it whets his appetites, which, in principle, can grow without measure. Moreover, and more importantly than is perhaps generally thought, the world of the nineteenth and twentieth centuries is not only possessed of all the perfection and amplitude of which it boasts, but it also insinuates to its inhabitants the deep-seated assurance that tomorrow will be even richer, more perfect, and more ample, as if it enjoyed a spontaneous, inexhaustible power of increase. Even today, despite signs which tend to breach the fabric of that robust faith, few people doubt that automobiles will be even more comfortable and cheaper in years to come. People believe this kind of thing as they believe that the sun will rise every morning. The meta-

---

* Formerly, because the world itself was poor, however rich an individual might be in relation to others, the range of facilities and commodities which his wealth procured him was still quite reduced. The life of the average man today is easier, more comfortable and secure than that of the most powerful of men in another age. What difference does it really make not to be richer than others, if the world itself is rich, and offers grand highways, transportation and communication, hotels, personal safety, and aspirin?

phor is an exact one. Because, finding himself in a world so socially and technically perfect, the common man feels that nature has produced it and never considers the personal efforts of highly-talented individuals which the creation of this new world presupposes. Still less would he admit that all these facilities continue to depend on the difficult skills of men and that a minimal break-down would cause the collapse of the whole magnificent structure.

These observations lead us to make two preliminary notations on our psychological diagram of today's mass-man: the unhindered expansion of his vital desires, that is, of his person or persona, and his total ingratitude toward all that has made possible the ease of his existence. These two traits together form the well-known psychological syndrome of the "spoiled child." It would not be erroneous to use this diagnosis as a key in examining the soul of today's mass-man. Heir to a long and genius-filled past, generous and genial in inspiration and effort, the new *vulgus*, the commonality, has been spoiled and indulged by the world around it. "To indulge" means to set no limits on desire, to further the impression that everything is allowed and that there are no obligations. Any creature nurtured on this regime will gain no experience of its own confines and limits. As a consequence of sparing it all external pressure, all restraint, every possible clash with others, it comes to believe in effect that it alone exists, and grows accustomed to not considering others, most especially to not considering anyone else as superior. This feeling for another's superiority could only come about through someone stronger who could cause our spoiled person to renounce some desire, to restrain or contain himself. Thereby that person could learn some fundamental discipline: "Here is the line where I end and where someone else, stronger than I, begins. In the world, apparently, there are two of us: me and someone superior to me." This elementary knowledge was taught everyman in past epochs, daily, by the world around him, for the world was so rudely organized that catastrophes were frequent, and nothing was sure, stable, or abundant. But the new masses find themselves in a secure prospect full of possibilities, everything placed at their disposal, without any previous effort on their part, in the way that we find the sun on high without our having carried it up on our backs. No human being thanks another for the air he breathes, inasmuch as no one has produced that air: it belongs to the sum of "what is there," of what we say "is only natural," for it is never lacking. The indulged modern masses are unintelligent enough to believe that our social and material organizations, placed at their disposal like the air, are of the same origin, since they, too, are apparently never lacking, and are almost as perfect as what is natural.

My thesis is this: the very perfection which the nineteenth century brought to the development and structure of certain orders of life has caused the masses who are the beneficiaries to think of this organization as a part of nature. We can thus define the absurd viewpoint of these masses: they are concerned only with their own well-being, and, at the same time, they show no concern for the causes and reasons for that well-being. They are uninterested. Since they do not see, behind the benefits of civilization, the marvels of invention and construction which made it possible and which can only be maintained by great effort and foresight, they imagine that their role is limited to demanding these benefits peremptorily, as if they were natural rights. In the past, when disturbances were provoked by a scarcity of food, the masses often concluded their search for bread by demolishing the bakeries. This may serve as a symbol of the public behavior which, on a vaster and more complicated scale, displays the attitude of the contemporary masses towards the civilization by which their standard of living is maintained.*

* Abandoned to its own inclinations, the mass, of whatever type it be, whether plebian or 'aristocratic', tends always, out of a pure zeal for life, to destroy the bases of its collective life. It has long

seemed to me that a telling caricature of this tendency, the tendency summed up in *propter vitam, vivendi perdere causas*, "in living one's life to lose one's reasons," is to be found in the events which occurred in Níjar, a town near Almería, when on September 13, 1759, Carlos III was proclaimed King. The proclamation was made in the city square. "Orders were issued to bring drink to the great multitude, which thereupon consumed 77 *arrobas* [616 gallons] of wine and four *pellejos* [skins] of hard liquor, which spirits so warmed them that with repeated rounds of 'Viva!' they set out for the public granary, from whose windows they hurled all the grain kept there, as well as 900 *reales* [silver coins] from its coffers. From there they moved on to the tobacco depot and emptied out the money for the monthly wages, as well as all the tobacco. They did much the same in the shops, pouring out all the wine and handing around all the foodstuffs in them, to give greater authority to the celebration. The ecclesiastic estate joined with equal efficacy, for they called out loudly to the women, urging them to throw from their windows all they had in their houses, which the women did with the greatest selflessness, to the point where they were left without bread, wheat, flour, barley, plates, pots, mortars, chairs, so that the village in effect was destroyed." This is the account given by a report written at the time, and cited in the *Reinado de Carlos III*, by Don Manuel Danvila (vol. II, note on p. 10). This town, then, so as to live out its monarchic joy to the full, annihilated itself. Admirable Níjar! To you belongs the future!

7

Noble Life and Common Life,
or Effort and Inertia

FROM OUR BEGINNINGS, we are that which our world invites us to be, and the fundamental features of our spirit are formed by the surrounding world as by a mold. Naturally so, for to live is to cope with the world around us. The general outline the world presents to us will be the general outline of our life. Hence my emphasizing the fact that the world in which the present-day masses originated possessed features radically new to history. Whereas in past times life for the average man meant difficulties, dangers, want, limitations on his destiny, and dependency, the new world makes its appearance as a sphere of practically limitless possibilities, a world of security in which one is independent of others. This primary and permanent impression is stamped on every contemporary soul, just as an opposite impression was stamped on those of prior times. For the basic impression becomes an interior voice which ceaselessly murmurs a message in the deeps of every soul and insinuates a definition of life which is at the same time an imperative. And if the traditional voice murmurs "To live is to feel limited, and therefore to feel a need to deal with the limitations," the newest and latest voice shrieks "To live is to deal with no limitation whatever. Therefore abandon thyself freely to thyself; practically nothing is impossible, nothing is dangerous and, in principle anyway, no one is superior to anyone else."

The make-up of the mass-man is completely modified, from its traditional, perennial pattern, by modern experience. In the past the common man always felt constitutionally bound by material limitations and by superior social powers. In his eyes, that was life. If he managed to improve his situation, he attributed his success to a lucky chance, favorable to him personally. And when he did not attribute it to luck, he knew it was due to enormous effort, the cost of which he well knew. In either case, it was a matter of an exception to the normal way of life and the world, an exception due to a very special cause.

But the new mass feels the full and free openness to life to be an established birthright, bestowed for no special reason whatsoever. Nothing external to itself suggests limitations, and there is no cause for it to refer to other experience, especially not to any of higher authority than itself. Not too far back in history, the average Chinese peasant believed that the well-being of his existence depended on the private virtues the Emperor was good enough to possess. Therefore, his life was lived in constant reference to the supreme authority on which it depended. *The man we are analyzing here, however, is accustomed to referring to no authority beyond his own*, certainly to none higher. He is satisfied with himself just as he is. Innocently, with no real need even to be vain, as if it were the most natural thing in the world, he will tend to affirm and consider as good whatever he finds in himself: his opinions, appetites, preferences, or tastes. Why not, since, as we have seen, nothing or nobody forces him to recognize that he is second-rate, highly limited, incapable of creating or conserving the very culture which furnishes him the fullness and amplitude upon which he bases his personal affirmations!

The mass-man would never have looked to a higher authority than himself, if *circumstances* had not violently forced him to do so. Inasmuch as circumstances now no longer force him to do so, the eternal mass-man, true to his nature, has ceased to look to other authority and feels himself lord of his own existence. The select man, the man of excellence, on the contrary, is impelled by his very nature to seek a norm higher and superior to himself, a norm whose authority he freely accepts.[1] At the very beginning we made a distinction between the common man and the select one, pointing out that the latter demands much of himself, while the other, requiring nothing of himself, is content with himself just as he is— delighted with himself, in fact.* Contrary to general belief, it is the man who demands excellence, and not the common man, who lives in essential servitude. For the select man, life lacks sense and savor unless he feels it serves a transcendental purpose. Thus he does not regard the need to serve as oppressive. When this need is lacking, through some chance, he feels restless and invents new and more difficult standards to spur him on. This is life lived as a discipline—the noble life. Nobility is to be defined by exigencies and obligations, not by rights.[2] *Noblesse oblige.* "To live at ease is plebeian; the noble mind aspires to ordinance and law" (Goethe). The privileges of nobility are not, originally, concessions or favors, but conquests. And their maintenance presupposed, in principal, that the privileged be ready to reconquer them, and to do so at any time, if necessary, and if challenged.† Private rights, or *privi-leges*, do *not* define passive possession and simple usufruct, but rather are meant to represent the contour of what personal effort achieves. On the other hand, common rights—such as "the rights of man, and of the citi-

---

* Any man who, in the face of any problem, is content to think whatever casually comes into his head, is intellectually part of the mass. On the other hand, the select man is one who gives little value to anything he finds without previous effort of mind, one who accepts as worthy only what yet lies beyond him and which requires a new extension of effort to be reached.

† See *España invertebrada* (1922), p. 156.

zen"—represent passive possession and pure usufruct, a generous gift of fate, ready-made for all men today, the result of no effort whatever, unless it be the effort of breathing or of avoiding insanity. Thus: an impersonal right is held, and a personal right is upheld.

The degeneration suffered in everyday language by an inspiring word like "nobility" is unfortunate. Since for many people it means "nobility of hereditary blood," it has become a category similar to common rights, that is, a static and passive quality, received and transmitted as if it were inert. But the proper sense, the *etymon*, the original literal meaning of the word "nobility" is essentially dynamic. "Noble" is *nobilis*, the known, the well-known, known to all the world, the notable one, who has made himself known by surpassing the anonymous mass. It implies a distinguished effort as cause for his fame. "Noble," then, is equivalent to "effortful," "excellent." When it comes to an heir, his nobility is pure benefit, no longer merit. The heir is endowed with the fame of his father. The glory is merely a reflection; hereditary nobility, in fact, is strictly indirect; it is mirrored light, it is a moon-nobility, derived from the dead. The only vital, authentic, dynamic quality left is the incentive for the descendant to keep up the level of effort achieved by the ancestor. Even in this impaired, diminished status, *noblesse oblige*, always. The original noble obligates himself, and the hereditary noble is obligated by his inheritance. In any case, there is a certain contradiction in the transfer of nobility from the initial noble to his successors. The Chinese, more logical, inverted the order of transmission, and it was not the father who ennobled the son, but the son who, by acquiring noble rank, communicated it to his forbearers, by his efforts ennobling his humble stock. Thus, in granting degrees of nobility, these are graded by the number of generations backwards which are to be honored: there are men who ennoble their fathers, and others who bestow their fame even unto their fifth or tenth great-grandfathers. The ancestors live by reason of a man in the present, whose nobility is activating, "in being," in *effect*. In short, it *is*, not *was*.*

"Nobility" does not appear as a formal term until the Roman Empire, and it appears precisely in opposition to the hereditary nobles, then in decadence.

To my mind, nobility is synonymous with a life of effort, ever set on excelling itself, intent always on going beyond what one is, to becoming what one proposes to be, as one's duty and obligation. Thus the noble life stands in contrast to common, inert life, which in a static way falls back upon itself, condemned to perpetual immobility, unless compelling circumstances, *force majeure*, make it come out of itself. Hence we use the term mass-man for that way of being man: not so much because this man is myriad, but because he is *inert*.

As one's existence evolves, one comes to realize more and more that the majority of men — and of women — are incapable of any effort beyond the one strictly imposed on them by a reaction to external necessity. For that very reason the few persons we come to know in our experience who are capable of spontaneous and joyous effort stand out as isolated, monumental. These few are the select men, the nobles, the ones who are active and not reactive, for whom life is perpetual tension, an incessant training. Training = *askesis*. And they are the ascetics.†

This apparent digression should cause no surprise. In order to define today's mass-man, who is as much mass-man as ever, but who now wants to supplant the select man, it is

* As we are here simply retracing the word "nobility" back to its original meaning, which excludes any question of inheritance, we do not touch on the fact of how often a "nobility of blood" occurs in history. We leave that matter aside.

† See "El origen deportivo del Estado" in *El Espectador*, Vol. VII.

necessary to counterpose him to two undiluted forms which in him are diluted: the eternal mass and the noble.

We can then proceed more rapidly, for we are now in possession of what to my mind is the key, the psychological equation, of the human type dominant today. Whatever follows is a consequence or corollary of the root-structure, which may be summed up thus: the world, as organized by the nineteenth century, automatically produced a new man, and in doing so provided him with formidable appetites and powerful means of every kind for satisfying them. These included the economic and the physical (hygiene, and the average level of health superior to that of all past times), the civil and technical (by which I mean the enormous quantity of partial knowledge and practical efficiency possessed by the average man today, always unavailable to such a man in the past). Having supplied him with all these powers, the nineteenth century abandoned him to himself, and the average man, true to his natural bent, has shut himself up within himself. In this wise, we are confronted with a mass stronger than in any epoch, but, differing from the traditional mass in its hermetical closure, incapable of heeding anyone or anything superior, in the belief that it is self-sufficient—in short, intractable, unteachable.* Continuing along this path, we shall soon see that in Europe, in the West, everywhere, the masses will prove unmanageable, unresponsive to any attempt at direction. In the difficult days ahead it is possible that, suddenly prey to anxiety and anguish, they may for a moment have the good faith to accept, in certain especially grievous matters, the direction offered by superior minorities.

But even this good faith will falter and fail. For the basic texture of their souls is wrought of hermetic intractability; from birth they lack the faculty of heeding anything or any-

---

* I have already spoken of the unruliness of the masses—especially of the Spanish masses—in *España invertebrada* (1922), and I refer to what was said there.

body outside themselves, whether facts or people. They will want to heed, and will be unable. They will want to hear, only to discover they are deaf.

On the other hand, it is illusory to imagine that the average man of today, however high his level in comparison to the average man of other times, will be able to control by himself the process of civilization. I say process, and not progress. The simple process of maintaining our civilization is supremely complex and requires incalculable subtlety. He is in no way fitted to direct it, this average man who has learned much of the apparatus of civilization but who is radically ignorant of its very principles.

I again suggest to the reader that he not give undue political significance to what has been stated above. Political activity, which is the most practical and obvious part of public life, is also the final product of other, more subtle and impalpable activity. Thus, political intractability would not be so serious if it did not follow from and indicate a more deep-rooted and decisive intellectual and moral intractability. For that reason, until we have analyzed these root-causes, our thesis will lack final clarity.

8

Why the Masses Intervene in Everything and Why They Always Intervene Violently

I TAKE IT THAT we can agree that something extremely para-doxical has come about; something, moreover, that was al-together natural. The opening up of life and of the world for the mediocre man has led him to shut up his soul. Now, I hold that it is this obliteration of the average soul that con-stitutes the gigantic problem facing humanity today.

Naturally many of my readers do not think as I do. That, too, is most natural and serves to confirm my thesis. For even if my opinion proved to be definitively erroneous in the end, the fact would still remain that many of the dissenting readers have never given five minutes' thought to this highly com-plex matter. How could they think as I do? But if they think they have a *right* to hold an opinion on the matter without previously working one out, without forging one, they would prove themselves examples of the absurd type of being I have called "the rebellious mass." Theirs is the way of the oblit-erated soul, hermetically closed: it is a case of intellectual hermetism. This kind of person finds himself with a fixed repertory of ideas. He decides to conform to these and thinks of himself as intellectually complete. Since he feels no need for anything outside himself, he settles back, content with his fixed repertory. Such is the mechanism of obliteration.

The mass-man regards himself as perfect. The select man,

in order to feel such perfection, would need to be exceedingly vain; belief in his perfection would not be a substantive part of him, nor would it be ingenuous, but would merely be an adjunct to his vanity, and even then would be fictitious, imaginary, problematic. The vain man would have need of others and would seek in them support for the idea he would like to have of himself. So that not even in this morbid case, not even blinded by vanity, does the noble man truly feel himself complete. On the other hand, the mediocre man of our time, the New Adam, is never in doubt about his completeness. His confidence, like Adam's, is paradisiacal. The inborn hermetism of his soul prevents him from discovering his insufficiency by comparing himself with others. To compare he would have to step out of himself and transpose himself into his neighbor. But a mediocre soul is incapable of transmigrations — the supreme sport.

We are faced, then, with the eternal difference between the wise man and the fool. The wise man is ever on the point of finding himself within an inch of becoming a fool, and so he makes an effort to escape from imminent folly, and in that effort lies his intelligence. The fool, on the other hand, harbors no suspicion about himself; he sees himself as being sharp, hence the enviable tranquility with which the fool accepts himself and settles into his foolishness. Like those insects which cannot be extracted from the orifice they inhabit, similarly there is no way of dislodging the fool from his folly, of leading him out of his blind self-rapture and of forcing him to compare his habitual dull vision with more subtle vision. The fool is a fool for life. There's no reaching him; he's impenetrable. That is why Anatole France said that a fool is much worse than a knave, for a knave sometimes lets up, the fool never.*

* I have often asked myself why, although for many men one of the greatest torments of their lives must have been their contact and clash with the folly around them, why, nevertheless, there has

It is not a question of the mass-man's being a fool. On the contrary, he is more clever, today, and more alert than his counterpart in any other era. But this new capacity is of no use to him; in fact, the vague feeling that he is clever serves only to make him more hermetic and to keep him from using his new capacity. Once and for all he is confirmed and con-secrated in his ready-made mentality; enthroned in his flow of commonplaces, stereotyped prejudices, empty words, and trite expressions; happy with all the loose ends with which his head is stuffed. And this mixture he expounds and imposes wherever he can, with a crass brazenness which only his simple-mindedness can explain. Herein is the point made at the outset of this work as to the characteristic of our epoch: not that the ordinary man declares himself super-excellent and not ordinary, but that the ordinary man proclaims his mediocrity and seeks to impose the right to be ordinary and claims commonplace vulgarity as a right.

The authority, the virtual hegemony exercised over public life by intellectual vulgarity is perhaps the most novel aspect of the present, the least like anything in the past. In any case, in the course of European history to date, the commonalty had never bethought itself to have "ideas" on everything. It possessed beliefs, traditions, experiences, proverbs, mental habits, but never considered that it needed to have theoreti-cal views on the way things are or ought to be—in politics or literature, for example. The projects of political leaders struck the masses as good or bad; they gave or withheld their sup-port, but their attitude was a reflection, an echo, positive or negative, of the creative activity of others. It never occurred to them to counterpose their own "ideas" to those of the political leader; nor did they venture to judge the political "ideas" of the leaders from the tribunal of their own pro-

---

never been a study of this conflict—an *Essay on Folly*? For the pages of Erasmus do not deal with the theme. [The 1979 edition of *La rebelión de las masas* omits the last sentence.]

jected "ideas." And the same held true regarding art and other aspects of public life. An innate awareness of their limitations, of their incapacity to theorize,* completely prevented it. The automatic consequence of this situation was that it did not occur to the masses, even remotely, to decide on public matters which are, for the most part, theoretic in nature.

Today, on the other hand, the average man possesses the most exact and circumstantial ideas on everything which occurs, and ought to occur, in the universe. And for this reason he has lost all ability to listen, has lost the use of his hearing. Why should he listen, when he has all the answers, everything he needs to know? It is no longer the season to listen, but on the contrary, a time to pass judgment, to pronounce sentence, to issue proclamations. There is no public question upon which he, stone-deaf and blind as he is, does not intervene and impose his "opinion."

But is this not an advantage? Does it not represent enormous progress that the masses should have "ideas," that is, that they should be cultivated, "cultured"? By no means. The "ideas" of this average man are not genuine ideas at all, nor does their possession mean culture. To have an idea is to put truth in check, in a checkmate position. Whoever wants to have ideas must be disposed to want truth and to accept the rules of the game which truth imposes. There is no use speaking of ideas or opinons if there is no acceptance of a process which authorizes and regulates them, of a series of norms and standards to which appeal can be made. These norms are the principles of culture, whatever form they take. What I affirm is that there is no culture where there are no norms and standards to which our fellow citizens can have recourse. There is no culture where there are no principles of civil legality to which to appeal. There is no culture where there is no accep-

---

* There is no use trying to get away from the fact that to state an opinion is to theorize.

tance of certain ultimate intellectual positions as points of reference in case of dispute.* There is no culture where economic relations are not subject to protective rules of conduct. There is no culture where aesthetic controversy does not recognize the necessity for justifying the work of art.

When all these necessities are lacking, there is no culture. There is, in the strictest sense of the word, barbarism. And—let us have no illusions—*that* is what is beginning to appear under the progressive rebellion of the masses. The traveler who arrives in a barbarous country soon learns that there are no ruling principles to which he may appeal in that place. Properly speaking, there are no barbarian norms. Barbarism is the absence of norms and of any possible appeal based on them.

The degree of culture is measured by a greater or lesser precision of standards and norms. Wherever there is little precision, the standards govern life only in a general manner, *grosso modo,* in an approximate way. Where there is a great deal of precision, standards govern the exercise of all activity.†

Outrageous political movements began in Europe long ago: one need only recall early aberrations like Spanish Syn-

---

* If in the course of controversy, someone shows no concern for conforming to truth, no desire to seek truth, that person is a barbarian. And lack of interest in truth is the attitude of the mass-man whenever he speaks, lectures, or writes.

† The paucity of intellectual life, that is, of cultivation or disciplined exercise of the intellect, is made manifest, not by greater or lesser knowledge, but rather by the habitual lack of care in adjusting to the truth, a habit so often displayed by intellectuals. It is not a matter of being right or not, of judging correctly—the attainment of truth is not in our hands—but of the lack of scruple and care to abide by the elementary requirements of sitting in judgment at all, let alone judging correctly. The Spanish, for example, still act like the eternal village priest who triumphantly refutes the Manichean without having troubled to ascertain what the Manichean thinks.

dicalism or Italian Fascism.[1] They were not strange simply because they were new. The lust for novelty is so innate in Western man that the European has already produced the most unsettling chapter in all history. What is strange about such developments is not their novelty so much as the extraordinary form in which they appear. The Fascist and Syndicalist species were characterized by the first appearance of a type of man who *did not care to give reasons or even to be right*, but who was simply resolved to impose his opinions. That was the novelty: the right not to be right, not to be reasonable: "the reason of unreason."[2] Here we can already see the most obvious manifestation of the new mentality of the masses. And it is due to their having determined to rule society without the capacity to do so. The structure of the new mentality is revealed, most crudely and tellingly, in their political conduct. Still, the key to it all lies in what we have called intellectual "hermetism." The mass-man finds himself loaded with "ideas," but he lacks the faculty to ideate. He does not even suspect the existence of the rare atmosphere in which ideas are bred and live. He wants to express opinions, but he does not wish to accept the conditions and requisites for having ideas to express. As a result, his "ideas" are no more than appetites expressed in words, as in the lyrics of musical comedy.

To have an idea is to believe that one has reasons for having it, and thus to believe that reason exists. It is to believe in reason and its world of intelligible truths. To have ideas, to form opinions, is to have recourse to some authority, to accept it and its code, its judgment and ruling, to believe that this highest form of social intercourse is a dialogue in which the reasons behind ideas are examined. But the mass-man would feel lost in such an examination, and instinctively rejects the obligation to accept any higher authority than himself. Thus, the "new" development in Europe was "to have done with discussion." There was a wave of reaction against any form of social intercourse which implied an obligation to abide by objective norms, whether in conversation or in parliament or in science itself. That meant a rejection of a way of life based on culture, which is a way of life involving norms, and there was a regression to barbarism. Normal interdependence was suppressed and recourse was taken to the direct imposition of whatever was most strongly desired. The hermetism of the soul which, as we have seen before, impels the mass to intervene in all aspects of public life, also drives it, inexorably, to a process of uniform intervention: "direct action."

When the origins of our epoch are pieced together, it will be seen that the first notes of its own particular melody were sounded by those groups of French Realists and Syndicalists, about the year 1900, who invented the method and even the phrase "direct action." Man has always had recourse to violence: sometimes the result is merely criminal, and that is not our concern here. But at other times it was the means resorted to by those who had previously exhausted all other means to preserve the rights to justice they thought they possessed or should possess. It may be regrettable that man's fate leads him over and over again to this form of violence, but it is undeniable that it also implies the greatest tribute to reason and justice. For this kind of violence is none other than reason exacerbated, driven to the limits of endurance and frustration. Force, violence, was, in effect, the *ultima ratio.* This phrase has been interpreted, rather stupidly, in an ironic sense. But it clearly expresses a resort to force after previous submission to *ratio*, to rational norms. Civilization is the attempt to render and reduce force to the *ultima ratio.* We can now see this with the utmost clarity, inasmuch as "direct action" inverts this order and proclaims force to be the *prima ratio*, and even the *unica ratio*, not only the *prime* form of reason, but the *only* form of reason. This is a norm to annul all norms, for it proposes the elimination of all others, and of all intermediate stages between our purpose and its imposition. It is the Magna Carta of barbarism.

It would be well to recall that whenever, in any epoch, the mass has taken action, for whatever motive, it has done so by "direct action." It has always been the natural procedure for the masses, their *modus operandi*, so to say. And this essay's thesis is strongly corroborated by the patent fact that now, when the dominant intervention of the masses in public life has gone from the infrequent and the occasional to the normal, "direct action" has officially become the recognized norm.

All communal life is beginning to fall under this new dispensation, in which indirect appeals are suppressed. In social relations, "good manners" no longer hold sway. Literature, as in "direct action," abounds with insult. Niceties are eliminated in sexual relations.

Niceties, norms, courtesy, mediation, justice, reason . . . What was the original point of such inventions, of creating all these subtle complications? They are all summed up in the word "civilization," which in its root, *civis*, "citizen," discloses its authentic origin. It is this concept which strives to make possible the city, the community, life in common. If we look into all the above-mentioned constituents of civilization, we shall find the same essence and purpose in each. All of them, in effect, presuppose a deep-rooted desire to count on each individual to take all others into consideration. Civilization is, above all, the will to live in concord. Barbarism is a tendency towards disassociation. Accordingly, all barbarous epochs have been times of human scattering, of the pullulations of minimal groups, cut off from and hostile to each other.

Liberal democracy represents, in political form, the loftiest will toward life in common, the most ample endeavor by man in this area so far. It carries to the furthest degree the resolve to count on each individual; it is the prototype of "indirect action." Nineteenth-century liberalism is the principle of political rights according to which the public power, though it be omnipotent, places limits on itself and attempts, even at its own expense, to leave a place in the state it governs for those who neither think nor feel like itself, that is, like those in power, like the majority. This liberalism, we should remember, is the supreme generosity: it is the right the majority grants to the minorities; it is, therefore, the noblest appeal to have been heard on this planet. It proclaims the determination to live with an enemy and, even more, with a weak enemy. It was quite unlikely, almost unbelievable, that the human race should have arrived at anything so paradoxical, so noble, so . . . antinatural. No wonder that mankind should soon show signs of wanting to get rid of it. It proves too difficult an exercise to take root on earth.

Live with an enemy! Share our existence! Govern with the opposition! Is not such tender consideration already proving to be incompatible with us all? Nothing highlights the physiognomy and characteristics of our age better than the increasingly few countries where an opposition is allowed to exist. In almost all countries a homogeneous and compact mass utilizes its weight and presses upon public power, crushing every dissident group. The mass—behold its monolithic appearance!—does not wish to share life with those who are not part of it. It has a deadly hatred of anything that is not itself.

9

Primitivism and Technology

IT IS MOST IMPORTANT to point out that we are engaged in the analysis of a situation — the present situation — which is essentially ambiguous. Hence the initial suggestion that present-day drives, especially what we have called the rebellion of the masses, open out in two directions. Each direction not only allows, but also requires, a double interpretation, one favorable, the other unfavorable. This ambiguity is not in our mind, but is to be found in reality itself. It is not that one side appears to be good from one point of view and bad from another, but that in itself the present situation contains the two potentialities of mastery or of death.

There is no call to burden this essay with a metaphysics of history. Nevertheless, I am clearly constructing one on the subterranean foundation of previously expressed philosophical convictions. I do not believe in the absolute determinism of history. On the contrary, I believe that all life, including historical life, is composed of purely momentary instances, each relatively undetermined as far as the previous moment is concerned, so that in each of them reality hesitates, vacillates, marks time, runs in place, paws the ground, and is uncertain of which possibility to choose. This metaphysical wavering, this humming uncertainty, makes everything alive seem to vibrate tremulously.

The rebellion of the masses *could* in fact be the transition to an unprecedented new order of humanity; it also *could* be a catastrophe for human destiny. There is no reason to deny the reality of progress, but we must amend the notion that progress is a sure thing. It is more in accord with the facts to realize that there is no sure progress, no evolution without the threat of "involution" and retrogression. Everything, everything is possible in history: triumphal and indefinite progress as well as periodic regression. Because life, individual or collective, personal or historic, is the only entity in the universe which is co-substantial with danger and threat. Life is composed of ups and downs, replete with reversals, sudden change. It is, in every sense, drama.*

This truth, a truth in general, acquires special intensity in "moments of crisis"—such as the present. Thus, the symptoms of new behavior appearing nowadays under the present aegis of the masses, and which we have subsumed under the heading of "direct action," *may* very well presage future perfectibilities. It is evident that any ancient culture in its development drags along in its train worn-out tissues and no small load of callous matter, toxic residue, and obstacles to life. There are moribund institutions, still-surviving norms now

---

* Needless to say, scarcely anyone will take these sentences seriously. Even the best-intentioned will understand them to be metaphors, however close to home. Only a reader innocent enough to realize that he does not know what life really is, or even what it is not, will let himself be won over by the elementary sense of these words and he will be the one to *understand* them, whether they are right or wrong. Among the remainder there will be an effusive unanimity, with the sole difference that some will believe life is the existential process of a soul, and others that it is a succession of chemical reactions. The point will scarcely be advanced among hermetically sealed readers by my stating that an entire way of thought can be summed up in the following definition: the *primary, radical* meaning of the word *life* is made clear when it is used in the sense of biography and not of biology. And this is true for the very good reason that any biology, in the end, is only a chapter in certain biographies, whatever biologists do in the course of their biography. Any other notion is abstraction, fantasy, myth.

grown meaningless, unnecessarily complicated solutions, standards demonstrably unrealistic. All these components of civilization, of "indirect action," call for a period of intense simplification. Contemporary shirt sleeves and casual dress take their revenge on the top hat and frock coat of the Romantic era. Simplification here is carried out in the name of health and taste: like all simplifications, it offers a better solution, where less means more. The tree of romantic love also was in need of pruning so as to bring down the load of false magnolias strung along its branches, and to cut away the riot of climbers, creepers, and tortuous ramifications which deprived it of sunlight.

Public life in general, and political life in particular, needed to be brought back to reality, to authenticity. European humanity could not take the leap called for by the optimistic enthusiasts unless it first shed its clothes, until it got down to bare essence, until it was at one with itself. The discipline of stripping bare, of getting back to the real self, is indispensable for clearing the way toward a worthy future. One must also claim full freedom of thought concerning the entire past. The future must prevail over the past, and it is the future which will determine our attitude toward that past.*

The great sin of omission of those in command during the nineteenth century must be avoided at all costs: their defective sense of responsibility and their consequent failure to maintain their guard. They allowed themselves to take the

* This freedom of attitude toward the past is no part of petulant rebelliousness; on the contrary, it is an evident obligation in every "critical epoch." A defense of the liberalism of the nineteenth century against the masses who attack it without civility does not mean a renunciation of full freedom of thought as regards this same liberalism. And vice versa: the primitivism we have shown in its worst aspect is in a certain sense a *sine qua non* for every historic advance. See what I had to say about this several years ago in my essay "Biología y Pedagogia," *El Espectador*, III, "La paradoja del salvajismo."

easy way in all circumstances and to dull themselves to danger inherent even in the most favorable circumstance. And that is to fail in the mission of leadership, in the obligation to fulfill one's responsibility. Nowadays it is imperative to create an urgent sense of responsibility in those capable of feeling it. The dire features symptomatic of our times must be faced squarely. On striking a balance in our diagnosis, there is little doubt that the adverse factors far outweigh the favorable ones, if the calculation be made not so much as regards the present as to what these factors presage.

All the increased material possibilities which life has created run the risk of self-obliteration in the face of the most fearful dilemma in the destiny of the West. Let us restate it: the direction of society has been taken over by a type of man oblivious to the principles of civilization. He is oblivious not only to the principles of *this* civilization, or *that* civilization, but as far as we can judge today, of any civilization. He is obviously interested in automobiles, anesthetics, and all manner of sundries. And these things confirm his profound lack of interest in civilization itself. For all these things are merely products of civilization, and the passion he displays for them makes more crudely obvious his insensibility to the principles which made them possible. We need only mention the following fact: since the appearance of the *nuove scienze* or natural sciences — that is to say, since the Renaissance — the enthusiasm shown toward these sciences steadily increased with no sign of regression. More concretely: the proportionate number of people who dedicated themselves to pure research in the sciences was greater in each succeeding generation. The first instance of a retrogression in this proportion occurred in the first quarter of the twentieth century. It began to be more difficult to attract students into the laboratories of pure science. And this continues to be true as industry reaches higher stages of development, and just as people begin to feel ever-greater appetites for the machines and medicines developed by science.

A similar incongruity could be shown in art, morals, religion, political thought, and in everyday life.

What does such a paradox demonstrate? This essay is an attempt to prepare an answer. It demonstrates that the type of man dominant today is a primitive, a *Naturmensch* emerging within a civilized world. The world is civilized, but the inhabitant is not: he does not even see its civilization, but uses it as if it were a part of nature. The new man wants his automobile, and enjoys using it, but he thinks it is the spontaneous fruit of some Eden-like tree. His mind does not encompass the artificial, almost unreal nature of civilization, and the enthusiasm he feels for its instruments does not include the principles which make them possible. When I use the words of Rathenau to say that we are witnessing a "vertical invasion of barbarians," it might be thought, as usual, that this was merely a phrase. It is clear that these words may enunciate a truth or an error, but it is far from being a mere "phrase." In short, it is a formal definition which summarizes a complex analysis. Contemporary mass-man is truly a primitive who has emerged from behind the scenes onto the age-old stage of civilization.

There is much talk nowadays of the fabulous progress of scientific technology. But there is not sufficiently dramatic awareness, even among the best minds, regarding its future. Spengler himself, so subtle and profound—though so obsessed—strikes me as too optimistic on this matter. For he believes that our "culture" will be followed by an era of "civilization," by which he means primarily technical advance. Spengler's notion of "culture" and of history in general is so remote from the suppositions underlying this essay, that there is no point here in arguing over his conclusions. We can reduce both our viewpoints to a common denominator, and thus show our differences, only by leaping over the bulk and detail of his theories. Spengler believes that technology can endure even when all concern for the principles of culture has died out. I cannot bring myself to believe any such thing.

Technology is of the same substance as science. And science does not exist without concern for its pure state, for itself, and it cannot continue without concern on the part of people for the general principles of culture. If the fervor for pure science is deadened, as appears to be the case, technology can only survive for a time, for the time left in the carryover from the cultural impulse which begat it. We live with technical needs, but not *from* them. Technology neither nourishes itself, nor breathes of itself, nor is its own cause. It is rather a useful, practical precipitate of superfluous, impractical concerns.*

The point being made is that the current interest in technology guarantees nothing, and that the idea of progress itself or the continuation of technology guarantees less than nothing. It is true that technological achievement is one of the features of "modern culture," that is, of a culture characterized by a portion of science which is materially productive. Thus, in describing here the entirely new face given life by the nineteenth century, I was left with only two really new features: liberal democracy and applied science.† And once again I must reiterate my astonishment at the way the vital

---

* Hence it seems clear that those who tell us that the United States can be defined by its 'technology' are telling us nothing. The mass of puerile judgments made on the United States in Europe is one of the most perturbing aspects of European thinking, especially when even the most cultured people are prone to them. It is a particular instance of the disproportion between the complexity of present-day problems and the capacity of our minds to deal with them.

† Liberal democracy and technology mutually imply each other, so much so that one is scarcely conceivable without the other; so that another, generic, name for them both together would be desireable, a third term to include them both. Such a term would constitute the real name, the substantive name for the past century and earlier.

connection between applied science and pure science is forgotten, as well as the fact that the conditions for the former's perpetuation are the same as those which made pure scientific activity possible. Has serious thought been given to all the prerequisites of mind and soul needed to assure that true "men of science" continue to exist? Can anyone seriously believe that science will exist as long as there are *dollars*? That kind of self-tranquilizing thought or mental pap is one more proof of primitivism.

What a quantity of ingredients of the most disparate nature must be brought together and shaken up to concoct the "cocktail" of physico-chemical science! Even the most cursory glance will reveal with the utmost clarity that in the width and breadth of the earth and of time, physics and chemistry came into being and initially established themselves in the limited quadrilateral formed by London, Berlin, Vienna, and Paris, and even in that small quadrilateral only as late as the nineteenth century. Experimental science, then, is one of the most improbable developments in history. Necromancers, priests, warriors, shepherds have come and gone and come again throughout history. But the fauna of experimental man apparently requires simply to come into being a combination of circumstances more exceptional than those which engender the unicorn. Such a bare fact, sobering indeed, should cause anyone to reflect a little on the super-volatile, evaporative nature of scientific inspiration.* Some visionary, indeed, the man who believes that if Europe disappeared, the Americans alone would see to the continuation of science!

It would be most important to study all this in depth, to specify in detail the historically vital presuppositions of experimental science and, consequently, of applied science.

---

* We avoid speaking here of deeper, more internal problems. As, of the fact that the majority of scientific researchers themselves do not have the slightest suspicion of the highly dangerous crisis which besets science from within at this time.

But let no one hope that, even if the question were clarified, the mass-man would see the point. The mass-man pays scant attention to reason, he learns only from what he feels in the flesh.

This situation gives one pause and inhibits any illusions about setting forth arguments which, because they would be based on reason, would have to be subtle. For, is it not absurd on the face of it that the mass-man, given the present level of development, is not profoundly moved, is not spontaneously aroused, by the existence of the physical and biological sciences? The situation is patent: while all other orders of culture — art, political theory, social conduct, morality itself — have become problematical, the efficacy of one activity is demonstrated daily before the eyes of the mass-man: that of empirical, applied science. It offers a new invention every day, something the common man can use. Every day produces a new analgesic or vaccine for the benefit of the average man. Everyone knows that if the number of laboratories were increased threefold or tenfold (and as long as scientific inspiration did not flag) there would be an automatic multiplication of wealth, comforts, health, prosperity. Could any better, more convincing propaganda in favor of a vital principle be imagined? How is it, then, that there is no sense on the part of the masses of the need to devote funds and interest for the better endowment of science? Far from it: ever since the first post-war period in this century the man of pure science has been converted into a sort of pariah. I speak of theoretical physicists, chemists, biologists — not of philosophers. Philosophy needs no protection, nor attention, nor sympathy, nor interest on the part of the masses. Its perfect uselessness protects it,* frees it from any subservience

* Aristotle *Metaphysics* 893a 10. [*Metaphysics* 893a 10 is a misprint in the Spanish editions, since, § 893a is in the *Problemata*. *Metaphysics* 983a 10 reads: "All the sciences, indeed, are more necessary than this, but none is better" (Ross trans.).]

to the common man. It knows well enough that it is in essence problematic, and joyously embraces its free destiny like a wild bird on the wing, with no need to ask anyone for anything, with no need to tout itself or defend itself. If someone can make use of it for anything, it sympathetically rejoices in the fact. But it does not live from benefits provided to others, nor does it take such considerations into account, or expect them. How could it expect anyone to take it seriously when it begins by doubting its own existence, when it lives only in the measure that it wages war on itself, in the measure that it unravels and undoes itself? Let us leave philosophy to one side, then, for it is an adventure of another order.

But the experimental sciences do need the mass-man, just as the mass-man needs them, under penalty of succumbing, inasmuch as without physics and chemistry this planet could not sustain the number of human beings which now inhabit it.

What arguments in favor of science can be better than those offered by the automobiles, in which the masses come and go, and the drugs which, *miraculously*, take away their pains? The disparity between the constant benefit which science offers and the interest shown by the beneficiaries is such that no one can fool himself with illusions: only barbarism can be expected from these beneficiaries. *Especially since this disdain for science as such is displayed with greatest impunity by the mass of technicians themselves, including doctors, engineers, and so on.* These latter customarily exercise their professions in the same state of mind as those who are content to use their automobiles or buy their bottles of aspirin—without the slightest real concern for the destiny of science or of civilization itself.

There are doubtless those who are more disturbed by other symptoms of emerging barbarism because these are of a positive nature, acts of commission rather than of omission, and which take place before our eyes and become spectacles. For me, the disparity between the benefit the common man receives from science and the respect he shows — or rather does *not* show — for science, that disparity is the most terrifying aspect.* I can explain this lack of adequate response by recalling that the Negroes of central Africa also drive around in automobiles and dose themselves with aspirin. The Western mass-man who is *beginning* to predominate is obviously, *relative to the complex civilization* into which he is born, no more than a primitive, a barbarian appearing on the stage through the trap-door, a "vertical invader."

---

* This monstrosity is increased a hundredfold by the fact that, as I have said, all the other vital principles of culture are in some disarray: the arts, law, political theory, religion, morality. While all are in temporary crisis at least, only science alone is not yet failing. On the contrary, it bears fruit daily, fabulously so, and yields even more than it promises. There are no grounds, therefore, for explaining the common man's disdain for it by imagining he is distracted by enthusiasm for some other form of culture.

10

Primitivism and History

NATURE IS ALWAYS with us, it is always *there*. It is self-sustaining. In the forests of nature we can be savages with impunity. We can go on being savages, with no danger other than that posed by the appearance on the scene of others who are not savages. Still, in principle, perennially primitive peoples are always possible. And they do exist. Breysig has called them "the peoples of perpetual dawn."[1] They have remained frozen in a motionless twilight, and their dawn never moves toward high noon.

All this can occur in a world which is pure nature. It cannot happen in the world of civilization, which is our world. Civilization is *not* always with us. It is not self-sustaining. Civilization is artificial and requires an artist or an artisan. If you want the fruits of civilization but do not care to cultivate and nurture it—you are fooling yourself. In a trice, you can be left without civilization. A moment of carelessness, and when you next look around you will find everything vanished into thin air! Just as if the tapestries you had hung to cover nature had suddenly been removed, and the primitive jungle had reappeared. The jungle is always primitive. And, vice versa, everything primitive is jungle.

Romantics of all epochs have been titillated by scenes of ravishment, in which the pallid form of woman is violated by the subhuman, and so they painted the swan overcoming the shuddering Leda, the bull covering Pasiphae, and Antiope

under the goat. In a general way, they found a subtly indecent attraction in a landscape with ruins, where the geometric
stone of civilization is stifled in the embrace of wild natural
growth. When your refined romantic catches sight of a building, the first thing his eye looks for is the "yellow hedge-
mustard" over cornice and roof. For it proclaims that everything is earth, and that the jungle springs up everywhere
anew.

It would be ill-advised to laugh at the romantic. For he
also is right. Beneath these innocently perverse images there
lies an immense and eternal problem: the relation between
civilization and that which underlies it, nature—the relation
between the rational and the cosmic. I reserve the right,
therefore, to play the role of the romantic on some other,
more opportune, occasion.

But right now I am engaged in the opposite task. Our immediate goal is that of containing the invading jungle. The
"good European" must at present devote himself to an enterprise similar to that which confronted the Australian states:
that of stopping the prickly-pear from taking over and driving man into the sea. Sometime in the 1840s, a Mediterranean immigrant, faithful to his native scenery—Malaga?
Sicily?—took with him to Australia a little pot with a tiny
prickly-pear in it. A few decades later the Australian budget
was burdened with heavy levies raised for the war against the
prickly-pear, which had invaded the subcontinent and was
gaining ground at the rate of more than a square kilometer
a year.

The mass-man believes that the civilization into which he
was born and which he uses, is as spontaneous and self-
producing as nature herself, and, ipso facto, he becomes a
primitive. He chooses to think of civilization as a jungle. I
have said this before, but now we must be more specific.

The principles upon which the civilized world rests, a
world we must maintain with our effort, do not exist for the
average man today. He is not interested in the fundamental

values of our culture, he does not feel any solidarity with
them, he is not inclined to place himself at their service. How
has all this come to pass? The reasons are numerous: for the
moment I will dwell on one.

As it advances, civilization becomes ever more complex
and difficult. Today's problems are intricately complicated.
The number of people with minds equal to the situation
grows smaller and smaller. Postwar periods have offered us
examples of this phenomenon. The reconstruction of Europe
after its wars has always been too algebraic a matter, and ordinary men are not up to intricate undertakings. There is no
lack of solutions, but there is a dearth of minds to find them.
More exactly, there are some clear heads, very few, but the
plebeian body of Europe does not want this kind of head on
its shoulders.

The disparity between the subtle complexity of the problems and the minds to deal with them will grow as long as
the gap is not closed. Herein lies the basic tragedy of our
civilization. The very fertility and surety of the formative
principles of our culture ensure a quantitative production of
material goods, to the point where production overflows the
receptive capacity of the ordinary man. I do not believe such
a situation has ever occurred in the past. All previous civilizations have perished from an insufficiency of resources. European, Western civilization is threatened by the opposite. In
Greece and Rome it was not man who failed, but his resources. The Roman Empire foundered from lack of applied
technique, that is, technology. When the population expanded, requiring solutions to problems of survival, solutions which only applied techniques could supply, the ancient world faltered, and there began a process of involution,
retrogression, and self-annihilation.

But now it is man who fails, since he is unable to keep pace
with his own civilization's progress. It is painful to hear the
most cultured people speak about the elementary problems
of the day. They resemble rough country bumpkins trying

with thick clumsy fingers to pick up a needle lying on a table. Political and social themes are handled with the dull conceptual instruments which were used two hundred years ago in situations two hundred times less complex.

An advanced civilization means complex problems. And the greater its progress the greater the threat under which it lives. Life gets better all the time, but also more complicated at every level. The means of solving the complexities are also perfected, but each generation must learn to use the improved means. The most obvious advantage is that each stage of advance is accompanied by an increase of experience: in short, of history. Historical knowledge is a first-rate instrument for preserving and continuing an already advanced civilization, not because it offers positive solutions to the new face of things — life is always different from what it was — but because it helps us avoid the innocent mistakes of past times. But if, in addition to being old and, therefore, beginning to find life difficult, one loses his memory of the past, and does not profit by experience, then everything becomes a disadvantage. And such is the condition in which Europe finds itself. The most "cultured" people today suffer from an incredible ignorance of history. I hold that contemporary Western leaders know much less of history than those of the eighteenth century, even less than those of the seventeenth century. The historical knowledge on the part of the governing minorities — "governing" *sensu lato*, in the wider sense — in those centuries made possible the prodigious advances of the nineteenth century. Political theory had been thought out — in the eighteenth century — precisely to avoid the errors of all previous policies. It had been thought out *in view* of those errors, and in its substance it condensed a vast amount of experience. But the nineteenth century had already begun to lose "historical culture," even though contemporary specialists developed history as science.* This loss, this neglect, is

* Here we already catch a glimpse of the difference between the state of the sciences in a given epoch and the state of its culture.

the source of many of the century's curious errors, which to-day weigh upon us. In the last third of the nineteenth century there began, though unperceived, a process of involution, a retrogression towards barbarism, that is, toward the ingenuousness and primitivism of those who have no past, or have forgotten it.

Hence, the two "new" ventures in politics that developed in Europe and around its borders in modern times are bolshevism and fascism, two clear examples of absolute regression. And they are regressive not so much because of the positive contents of their doctrines, which in isolation contain some partial truth, naturally—for who in the universe does not possess some particle of truth?—but because of the anti-historical, anachronistic manner in which they treat their particle of truth. Both of them are movements typical of mass-men, led, as all such movements are, by mediocrities, extemporaneous men with short memories, with no "historic consciousness," who behave from the start as if they were already part of the past, as if they belonged to the fauna of a previous age.

It is not a question of being or not being a communist. I am not discussing their creed. What is inconceivable and anachronistic is that a communist, a Bolshevik, should help launch a revolution in 1917 identical in form to all those that have ever been and in which not a single error or defect of previous revolutions has been corrected in the slightest. For that reason, what has happened in Russia is of no historical interest. And hence, it is exactly the opposite of a new beginning for human life. On the contrary, it is a monotonous repetition of the revolution of always, the eternal revolution. It is the perfect commonplace of revolutions, a cliché. So much so, that there is no stock-phrase or stereotype, among the great store accumulated by human experience with revolution, which does not find dreadful confirmation in the Russian Revolution. "Revolution devours its own children!" and "Revolution starts with a moderate party, passes at once to extremists, and soon begins to retrogress toward a restoration . . . " and so on. To these venerable commonplaces some other lesser known truths might be added, as: a revolution does not maintain itself pure for more than fifteen years, a period of time in which a new generation comes into its own.*

Whoever truly aspires to create a new social or political reality must first of all make sure that these most common of commonplaces of historical experience be rendered outdated by the situation he helps bring into being. For my part, I shall reserve the title of "political genius" for the office seeker who begins his campaign by driving professors of history mad, as they behold the "laws" of their science become dated, outmoded, reduced to a pile of rubble.

If for bolshevism we substitute fascism, we could say much the same for it. Neither improvisations are up to "the level of our times," for they do not encompass or represent the past in foreshortening, and that is an essential condition for improving on that past. One does not engage the past in hand-to-hand combat. The future overcomes the past by swallowing it. If the future leaves anything of the past outside itself, it is lost: the future is lost.

Bolshevism and fascism are pseudo-dawnings, altogether false dawns. They do not presage the morrow of a new day, but that of an archaic day, a day already done and spent a

---

* A generation has an active life of about thirty years. Its activity is divided into two stages and takes two forms: during the first half, approximately, the new generation propagates its ideas, preferences, and tastes, and these take over and set the tone for the second half of its course. But the generation brought up under its aegis embodies other ideas, preferences, and tastes, which begin to be diffused. Whenever the ideas, preferences, and tastes of the dominant generation are extremist in nature and revolutionary, the new generation tends to be antiextremist and counterrevolutionary, that is, it favors restoration in general. 'Restoration' does not of course mean a simple 'return to the old ways,' something restorations have never really accomplished.

thousand times. They represent primitivism. They are like all movements which stop to battle with some portion of the past instead of proceeding to digest it.

There is no doubt that we must move beyond the liberalism of the nineteenth century. But that is precisely what cannot be done by any such thing as fascism, which proclaims itself antiliberal. For that is what man was and did before liberalism existed: he was antiliberal or nonliberal. Inasmuch as liberalism already triumphed over the latter, it will either go on being victorious or everything will come apart — liberalism and antiliberalism — in the destruction of Europe. An inexorable chronology prevails. Liberalism is posterior to antiliberalism, or, what amounts to the same thing, is more vital than the latter, just as the cannon is more of a weapon than the lance.

At first sight, any attitude involving an *anti-* seems to be posterior to whatever it is *anti-*, since it signifies a reaction against the thing in question and thus supposes the latter's previous existence. But the innovation represented by the *anti-* soon fades into an empty attitude of negation and its only positive element is something *antique*. Whoever proclaims himself to be anti-Peter or Paul simply declares himself a believer in a world where Peter or Paul do not exist. But that was precisely the state of the world before Peter or Paul were born. The anti-Peter or anti-Paul-ist, instead of placing himself after Peter or Paul in time, places himself in a time before them, and runs the film back to a previous time, at the end of which Peter or Paul inevitably reappear. What happened in legend to Confucius happens to all those who are simply *anti-*: Confucius naturally was born after his father, but he was already eighty at birth, by Chinese ancestor-count, while his father had only been thirty at birth! Every cry of *anti-* is no more than a hollow *no*.

It would all be simple enough if with a good round *No!* we could wipe out the past. But the past is by nature a *revenant*. If it is cast away, it comes back anyway, it returns inevitably. Thus, the only way to supersede the past is to incorporate it. One must deal with the past, count on it, and thus go beyond it. In short, live "at the level of the times," in full consciousness of the historical juncture.

The past has its reasons, its own reasons. It is right, with its own rights. If it is not given its rights, it will reclaim them and, in the course of doing so, will exercise rights to which it has no right. Liberalism had its reason and rights, too, and they will have to be accepted *per saecula saeculorum*. But it was not altogether right, and what it did not have the right to impose must be taken from it. Europe needs to keep its essential liberalism. That is the necessary condition for superseding it.

These references to fascism and bolshevism have been merely oblique allusions, for the point made here is that they are each an anachronism. And this same characteristic is inseparable from everything that appears triumphant today. For it is the mass-man who triumphs now, and only projects initiated by him, saturated with his primitive views, are able to achieve apparent victories. Apart from all this, however, I am not discussing the essence of either manifestation, nor am I attempting to resolve the eternal dilemma between revolution and evolution. The most this essay ventures to ask is that revolution or evolution be historical and not anachronistic.

The theme I pursue in these pages is politically neutral, for it belongs to something deeper than politics and its dissensions. The conservative may be no less a mass-man than the radical, and their differences, which tend to be superficial through the years, do not prevent them from being one and the same man, a common man in rebellion.

Europe has no salvation unless its destiny is put in the hands of truly "contemporary" men who feel the pulse of history, of the entire past, and yet who know the "level of the times" and reject every archaic and primitive stance. We need the whole of history, history in its entirety, not to fall back into it, but to see if we can escape from it.

11

The Age of Self-Satisfaction

THE NEW SOCIAL phenomenon we have analyzed here makes clear that Western history appears, for the first time, to be handed over to the common man as such. History is now dependent on the decisions of mediocrities. Or, to put it in the active voice: the common man, hitherto directed from above, is now determined to govern the world. His determination to move into the foreground of the social scene came about, automatically, as soon as this new type of man came into being. If the psychological structure of this new mass-man is considered in regard to its social effect we find the following: 1) he is possessed of an inborn and deep-seated belief that life should be easy, plentiful, without tragic limitations; thus the average individual is animated by a sense of power and success which 2) leads him to affirm himself just as he is, and to consider himself complete in his moral and intellectual being. This self-satisfaction leads him to deny any exterior authority, to refuse to listen, to evade submitting his opinions to judgment, and to avoid considering the views of others. He is driven to make his weight felt. He will tend to act as if only he and his kind exist in the world; and thus 3) he will involve himself in everything, putting forth his mediocre view, without hesitancy, reserve, reflection, or negotiation. That is to say, his intervention will take the form of "direct action."

This series of features has made us think of certain defective types of humanity, such as the "spoiled child" and the primitive in revolt, that is, the barbarian. (The normal primitive, on the other hand, is the most submissive man known, to whatever authority, be it religion, social tradition, customs, taboo.) One need not be surprised at all the pejoratives with which I assail this form of humanity. The sharp attack made here on our present mass-man as ruler is no more than a first sally, a preliminary essay against this vulgar victor. Many Western thinkers are bound to take energetic issue with the mass-man's aspirations to tyrannize. For the present, we are content with this polemic as a skirmish; a frontal attack will inevitably follow in a far different form, one which the mass-man will not be able to avert, when he sees it unfold without realizing that it is a frontal attack.

This type of man, our modern mass-man, who is to be found anywhere and everywhere, inflicting his kind of barbarism on one and all, is really the spoiled child of history. The spoiled child is an heir who acts like an heir and nothing else. In this case the inheritance is civilization, with all its goods, conveniences, and security: in short, with all the advantages of civilization. As we have seen, only within the boundlessness of the material luxury which civilization has now created is such a mass-man possible: a man of this type can come into being only in the circumstance of easy existence, such as we have now achieved. It is one of many deformations produced by comparative luxury and overindulgence.

We might easily believe that a well-endowed world is necessarily better, that it implies a fuller life, one with more quality, than a life lived in constant struggle with scarcity. But that is not the case, for reasons of a most fundamental nature, which we need not analyze at this point. Instead of giving reasons it will suffice to cite the example of the age-old tragedy of every hereditary aristocracy. The aristocrat inherits, that is, he finds at hand certain qualities attributed to his person, none of which he has earned or created, none of which are organically part of his own personal life. At birth he finds himself already endowed, without delay and without his knowing why, with his wealth and prerogatives. He himself has nothing to do with all this, for none of it comes from within himself. These advantages are the armor, the gigantic shell of another person, of some other being—his ancestor. And the heir must live *as* heir. That is, he must use another man's armor. And so, what life is a hereditary "aristocrat" to lead, his own or that of another man, that of the noble ancestor? Neither the one nor the other. He is condemned to *represent* the other man: consequently, *to be* neither the other man nor himself. Inevitably his life lacks authenticity and is converted into a sheer representation, a fantasy, of another man's life. The surplus of resources he is obliged to handle does not allow him to live his own life, fulfill his own destiny: his life becomes atrophied. *All life is the effort, the struggle to be itself.*

The difficulties you encounter in the course of living your life are precisely the ones which arouse and mobilize your drive and capacity. If your body did not weigh on you, you would not be able to walk. If the atmosphere did not press upon you, you would feel your body as something vague, amorphous, unsubstantial—a phantom. Likewise, for the hereditary "aristocrat," his whole being, his individuality, grows vague from lack of use and vital effort. The result is that special foolishness of the old nobility, which is like no other folly, and which has never yet been described in its inmost, tragic mechanism—the tragic mechanism which leads all hereditary aristocracy to inexorable degeneration.

We say this much merely to counter the innocent tendency to believe that a surplus of means is most favorable to life. Quite the opposite is the case. A world overabundant in possibilities* automatically produces grave deformities, vicious

---

* An increase or even an amplitude of means should not be confused with an overabundance. In the nineteenth century, the facilities of life were greatly increased, and this produced the prodigious growth—quantitative and qualitative—traced above. But the time

forms of human existence, such as the general type of "inheritance-man," of which the "aristocrat" is a particular example, as is the "spoiled child," and, in a broader and more radical way, the mass-man of our time. It would be easy enough to expatiate on the "aristocrat," to show how many of his characteristic traits, as they appear in all places and all times, reappear in the mass-man today. For instance, the propensity to make games and sports the central occupation of life; the cult of the body, with its health-regime and focus on the effect of clothes; the lack of romance in dealing with women; the habit of making light of academics and intellectuals and ultimately despising them; the preference for life under absolute authority to life guided by free discussion.*

It is necessary to emphasize, then, that the new man, so full of uncivil tendencies, this newest of barbarians, is the

has come when the civilized world, as regards the capacity of the average man, has reached *excessive* proportions, superabundance, superfluity. A single example of this: the security which seemed concomitant with progress (ever-increasing living advantages) only demoralized the common man, lending him an assurance which has by now proven false and atrophied.

* On this head, as on many others, the English aristocracy seems to be an exception to much of what we have said. Still, though their example may be most admirable, a brief sketch of British history would be enough to show that though it is an authentic exception, it confirms the rule. Contrary to what is generally held, the English nobility has been the least fortunately endowed of Europe and has lived in more constant danger than any other. And because of these factors it has always been able to make itself respected, which means it has stood untiringly on guard. It is often forgotten that England was, until well into the nineteenth century, the poorest country in the West. This fact saved the nobility. Since it was not overendowed in resources, it was forced to accept commercial and industrial occupation — something considered ignoble on the Continent. In short, it soon decided to live economically in a creative manner and not merely to count on its privileges.

automatic product of modern civilization, especially of the form this civilization adopted in the nineteenth century. This new man did not burst in on the civilized world from outside, like the "great white barbarians" of the fifth century; nor was he born within it by the mysterious spontaneous generation which, according to Aristotle, causes tadpoles to appear in a pond; he is, instead, an entirely natural product. It is possible to formulate a law confirmed by paleontology and bio-geography: human life has come into being only when the resources it could count on were in balance with the problems it encountered. This is as true in the spiritual order as in the physical. Thus, to refer to a most concrete aspect of corporal existence, it may be recalled that the human species has appeared and flourished in zones of our planet where the hot season has been compensated for by a season of intense cold. In the tropics, the human animal tends to degenerate, and, conversely, inferior races—the pygmies, for example— have been pushed toward the tropics by races born later in the time scale and superior in the scale of evolution.[*]

The civilization which began in the nineteenth century was of such an order that it allowed the average man to set himself up in a world characterized by abundance. The immediate result was that he perceived the abundance without encountering the age-old difficulties of man. He found himself surrounded by unprecedented inventions and medicines, by welfare states, and ample rights. He forgot the difficulties attendant on the invention of these implements and medicines, and the task of assuring their future production. He did not notice how unstable was the organization of the state and was scarcely conscious of any obligations on his own part. This imbalance leads to a falsification of man's nature, weakens his very roots, and causes him to lose contact with the substance of life, whose radically problematic condition is one of absolute danger. The most contradictory form of human life

* See Olbricht, *Klima und Entwicklung*, 1923.

is that of the "self-satisfied man," the spoiled child grown up. Whenever this type becomes predominant, the voice of alarm should be sounded, for life is then threatened with degeneration, that is, with approaching death. According to our view, the level attained by the West today is superior to any in the past as far as the average man is concerned, but if we look to the future, we find grounds to fear that it will neither preserve this level nor reach a higher one, but that, on the contrary, it may well regress to inferior levels.

It is easy to see the abnormality represented by the "self-satisfied man." For he is the man who has come into being to do what he feels like. This is the illusion which guides the *fils de famille*, the boy-heir to "a good family." We already know why: in the family circle, everything, even the worst faults, are in the long run left unpunished. The family circle is relatively artificial and countenances many an act which in society, in the world outside, would involve unavoidable and disastrous consequences for its author. But this type of man thinks he can behave outside as he does at home; he believes that nothing is irrevocable, irremediable, fatal. Hence he thinks he can do as he pleases.* And that's a great mistake! "Your excellency will go where they take you," the parrot is told in the Portuguese story. *"Vosa mercê irá a onde o levem."* The fact is that one not only *ought not* to do what one pleases, but that one cannot do other than what one *has* to do, and cannot be other than what one *has* to be. The only way out is to refuse to do what has to be done, but this negative action does not free us to do what we please. On this

* What the house is to society, the nation is on an even larger scale to other nations. One of the most telling manifestations of the 'self-satisfied complex' is the position assumed by some nations of doing whatever they please in the international community. They ingenuously call this attitude 'nationalism'. Though I detest all ritual submission to 'internationalism', I find absurd and detestable the flighty spoiled-child conceit displayed by the least-developed nations.

point we possess only the negative freedom of will, a *nolun-tas*, a nullitude or "nillitude." We can assuredly turn away from our true destiny. But that merely imprisons us at lower stages of that destiny. As regards the highly individual destiny of each of us, each individual is an unknown. It is evident, however, that some portion or facet of his destiny is similar to that of others. For example, every European today knows, with a certainty greater than that of all of his expressed "ideas" or "opinions," that he and all other Europeans *must* be liberal. We need not discuss what type of liberty he must espouse. I refer to the fact that even the most reactionary of Europeans knows, in the depths of his consciousness, that what was attempted by Europe in the last century under the name of liberalism was something which in the long run was fated, destined, inexorable, resulting in something which today's Western man *is*, whether he likes it or not.

Though it could be proved with incontrovertible evidence that all of the specific ways in which the attempt was made to carry out the imperative in European destiny—to be politically free—have been lamentable and misbegotten, the final evidence for the attempt shows it to have been *substantially* right for the nineteenth century. This *ultimate* evidence exerts its pressure equally on the European fascist or communist, whatever he may say or do to convince us or himself to the contrary, just as it is valid for the Catholic who gives his primary adherence to the *Syllabus.**[1] They all "know" that

* He who holds the Copernican *belief* that the sun does not fall on the horizon continues *to see it* fall, and since seeing implies a primary conviction, he continues *to believe it*. What occurs is that his scientific *belief* constantly arrests the effects of his primary or spontaneous belief. Thus it is that this Catholic denies, with his dogmatic belief, his own *authentic* liberal belief. The allusion to this Catholic merely serves as an illustrative example of the idea that I am expounding now. But the radical censure I direct at the mass-man of our time—at the "self-satisfied *señorito*"—does not refer to this Catholic. Rather it coincides with him only on one

beyond the justified criticism leveled against the manifestations of liberalism there remains an irrevocable truth attached to it, a truth which is not theoretical, intellectual, or scientific, but of an entirely different and more decisive order—it possesses the truth of destiny. Theoretical truths are not only open to discussion, but their very strength and sense lies in their being questioned: they are born in discussion, they live so long as they are being discussed, and are so formulated that they must be discussed. But destiny—which is what must in life be or not be—destiny is not a question of discussion but must be accepted or not. If we accept it, we are authentic; if not, we live a negation, a falsification of ourselves.* Destiny does not consist in what we feel like doing; rather, it is recognized by our being conscious that we *must* do what we do not feel like doing.

Now, the "self-satisfied" man can be defined as one who "knows" that certain things cannot be, but who pretends, by act and word, that the contrary is the case. The fascist will let himself be mobilized against political liberty knowing full

---

point. What I reproach in the self-satisfied man is the lack of authenticity in almost all his being. The Catholic is not authentic at some points of his being. But even this partial coincidence is only apparent. The Catholic is not authentic in one part of his being— all that he has, like it or not, of modern man—*because* he wants to be faithful to another real part of his being, his religious faith. This means that the destiny of that Catholic is in itself tragic. And by accepting that portion of inauthenticity, the Catholic does his duty. The self-satisfied *señorito*, on the other hand, frivolously and utterly deserts himself, precisely in order to avoid all tragedy.

* Abasement, degradation, is simply the only manner of life left to the man who has refused to be what he should be. His authentic being does not die, however, but becomes an accusing phantom which makes him forever feel the inferiority of the life he lives compared to the life he ought to have lived. The degraded man is a victim of suicide who has survived.

well that in the end it will survive in the West along with the
substance and essence of Europe, to reappear when it is criti-
cally and vitally needed. For this is the mark and keynote of
the mass-man: his lack of seriousness and his taste for buf-
foonery and farce. The actions of mass-man lack any sense of
irrevocability: they are like the pranks and escapades of rich
kids. Their penchant for adopting hard, pseudo-tragic attitudes is mere show. They play at tragedy because they think
the real tragedy of the civilized world is not to be believed.

We would be in a fine fix if we accepted as authentic
whatever view of himself a person tried to foist on us. If
someone were to insist that two plus two equals five, and if
there were no reason to suppose him insane, we may be sure
he does not really believe it, however much he may vocifer-
ate, and even if he vouches for it with his life.

Europe is shaken by a hurricane of farce. Almost all the
positions and stances taken are false. The only real effort expended is in fleeing one's own destiny, in shutting one's eyes
to its inevitability, in avoiding a face-to-face confrontation
with being *what one must be.* People live life as a comedy,
and the more tragic the mask, the more farcically they live.
Comedy prevails whenever ephemeral attitudes prevail, when
people do not stand fast. The mass-man will not stand up to
his destiny, to its unmovable presence; he vegetates while living a fictitious existence suspended in air. Never before have
there been such weightless, rootless, uprooted lives— *deracinées*
from their own destiny—floating on the slightest breeze, on
any current. This is the epoch of "currents," of "letting yourself go." Almost no one offers any resistance to the faddish
ephemeral whirlwinds which blow up in the world of art or
of ideas, or in politics or social customs. Consequently, rhetoric
is more common than usual. The "super-realist" feels he has
gone beyond all literary history when he writes down some
complicated excrescence where others wrote "jasmines, swans,
and fauns." What he has really done is to dredge up another
rhetoric which lay dormant in the latrines.

The present situation can be clarified by noting what, despite its peculiar features, it has in common with other periods. Thus, scarcely had Mediterranean civilization reached its peak—around the third century B.C.—when the cynic makes his appearance: Diogenes in his mud-covered sandals tramps over the carpets of Aristippus. The cynic appeared around every street corner and at all levels of society. In actual fact, the cynic did nothing but sabotage that civilization. He was the nihilist of Hellenism. He created nothing, he constructed nothing. His role was to undo, or rather, to attempt to undo, but he did not fulfill that task either. The cynic, civilization's parasite, lives by denying civilization, precisely because he is convinced, again, that it will not fall. What would the cynic do among a primitive people, where everyone, in all seriousness and altogether naturally, does what he believes to be his personal task? What is the role of a fascist if he does not inveigh against liberty, or of a super-realist if he does not inveigh against art?

Nothing else could be expected from the mass-man: he has been born into an overorganized world, of which he understands the advantages and not the dangers. He is spoiled by the world around him, by "civilization," which is his house and home, and this pampered child does not encounter anything to contravene his whims, to draw him out of himself, to make him listen to higher authority, and, even less, to plumb the depths of his own destiny.

12

The Barbarism of Specialization

OUR THESIS, then, is that nineteenth-century civilization auto-matically produced the mass-man. Before finishing our general exposition let us analyze a concrete example of the mechanics of this phenomenon, for in this way our thesis becomes more persuasive.

The civilization of the nineteenth century may be summed up in its two great dimensions: technology and liberal demo-cracy. Let us first consider the former. Modern technology is born from a union of experimental science and capitalism. Not all technology is scientific. The man or men who made stone axes in the Chellian age were devoid of science and yet they created a technique. China achieved a high degree of specialized technology without in any way suspecting the ex-istence of physics. Only the modern technology of Europe had a scientific root, which gave it a specific character and the possibility of unlimited progress. Other systems of technology— Mesopotamian, Egyptian, Greek, Roman, Oriental—achieved a point of development beyond which they could not go and, upon reaching that point, they began to retrogress into a rather pitiful involution.

Our splendid Western technology has made possible the proliferation of the European species. One need only recall the data which served as point of departure for our polemic, for it underlies all these reflections. From the fifth century to 1800, Europe never reached a population of more than 180 million. Then, from 1800 to 1914 it rose to more than 460 million. This jump is unique in human history. There can be no doubt that technology — together with liberal democracy — engendered the mass-man in the quantitative sense. But these pages attempt to show that it is also responsible for his existence in the qualitative and pejorative sense of the term as well.

By mass, as we said at the beginning, we do not primarily mean the working class. The term as used here does not designate a social class but a type of man to be found today in all social classes, who is representative of our age insofar as he plays a dominant role. We shall find abundant evidence of this predominance.

Who today exercises social power? Who imposes his kind of mind on the epoch? Without a doubt, the man of the middle class. Who, within that middle class, is considered the leading group, the aristocracy of the day? Without a doubt, the technician: the engineer, the physician. And within the group of technical men, who represents them in the highest and purest form? Quite clearly, the scientist. If a man from outer space were to visit Europe and were to ask, for purposes of judging our culture, which men were held in highest regard and by whom we preferred to be represented, we would surely offer, as the best example, our men of science. Clearly the man from outer space would not be seeking exceptional individuals, but would be looking, rather, for the generic "man of science," apex of European humanity.

Now, it so happens that today's scientist is the very prototype of the mass-man. Not by chance, nor because of any personal defects in individual men of science, but because science itself — the root of our civilization — automatically converts him into a mass-man. That is, it turns him into a primitive, into a modern barbarian.

This is a well-known fact; it has been demonstrated countless times; but in the context of this essay it may acquire its full meaning and gravity.

Experimental science had its beginnings at the end of the

sixteenth century with Galileo; it succeeded in establishing itself at the end of the seventeenth century with Newton; and began to expand in the middle of the eighteenth. The development of anything is always different from the stage when it was first established, for it is subject to different conditions. Thus in the establishment and constitution of physics—the collective name for experimental science—an effort at unification was required. Such was the task of Newton and his contemporaries. But the evolution and expansion of physics initiated a phenomenon whose nature is the opposite of unification. In order to progress, science required specialization, not in science, but in the scientists. Science is not by nature specialistic. If it were, it would *ipso facto* cease to be authentic. Not even empirical science, taken as a whole, can be true, if divorced from mathematics, from logic, from philosophy. But scientific *work* must, by necessity, be specialized.

It would be of great interest and utility to trace the history of the physical and biological sciences and to demonstrate the process of increased specialization in the work of investigators. One would see how, generation after generation, the scientist has gone on constraining and restricting himself to increasingly narrow intellectual concerns. But, that is not the most important point that this history reveals. What is most pertinent is that in each generation the scientist, because he must reduce the sphere of his work, progressively loses contact with other branches of science and with an integral interpretation of the universe, that is, with the only thing worthy of the names of science, culture, and Western civilization.

Specialization begins precisely at the point when the "encylopedic" man is considered to be the civilized man. The nineteenth century takes up its destiny under the aegis of men who lived "encyclopedically," though their work already shows signs of specialization. In the following generation, the balance is upset, and specialization begins to displace integral culture in every scientist. By 1890 a third generation takes command in the intellectual world, and we find a type of scientist without precedent in history. He is a person who knows, of all that a routinely dutiful man must know, only something of one specific science; even of this science, he is well informed only within that limited area in which he is an active researcher. He may even go so far as to claim that he has an advantage in not cultivating what lies outside his own narrow field, and he may declare that curiosity about general knowledge is the sign of the amateur, the dilettante.

Immured within his small area, he succeeds in discovering new facts, advances the science which he scarcely knows, and increases perforce the encyclopedia of knowledge of which he is conscientiously ignorant. How was this possible, and how is it still possible? We must face up to the extraordinary and undeniable fact that experimental science has in large part developed because of the work of men who were incredibly mediocre, and even less than mediocre. Modern science, root and symbol of our present civilization, provides plenty of room for the intellectually commonplace man and allows him the opportunity for successful work. And this is due to the factor which repesents the greatest advantage as well as the greatest peril in the new science and the civilization it represents: that is, mechanization. A fair amount of the work to be done in physics and biology is made up of mental work which is mechanical and which can be done by almost anyone. Endless research can be carried out by dividing science into small segments, allowing the individual to concentrate on one of these while ignoring the others. The exactitude of methods permits this temporary but practical dismembering of knowledge. Working with one of these methodologies is like working with a machine: one can obtain significant results without having any clear understanding of the fundamental meaning of the method itself. Thus the majority of scientists help the general advance of science even while confined each to his own little laboratory cell, working in the way the bee works in the cell of his hive.

All this creates an extraordinarily strange caste of men. The researcher who has discovered a new fact of nature, for instance, must necessarily experience a certain sense of authority and self-assurance. With a certain apparent justice he feels himself to be "a person who knows." And in all truth, he possesses a portion of something which, together with other portions of something not privy to him, constitutes knowledge. And here we have the true characteristic of the specialist, who in the twentieth century has achieved heights of the wildest self-importance. The specialist "knows" his own minimal corner of the universe quite well. But he is radically ignorant of all the rest.

In this strange type we have a splendid example of the new man whom we have tried to define in many of his different facets. We have pointed out that our mass-man is a type without parallel in history. The specialist serves as a striking, concrete example of his kind, and in him we see the root-nature of this novelty. Previously, men could be divided simply into the learned and the ignorant: some more or less learned, and some more or less ignorant. But the specialist cannot be subsumed under either of these two categories. He is not learned, for he is formally ignorant of all that does not fit into his specialty; but neither is he ignorant, for he is "a man of science," a scientist, and he knows his own sliver of the universe quite well. We shall have to call him a learned-ignoramus, which is a very serious matter, for it means that he will act in all areas in which he is ignorant, not like an ignorant man, but with all the airs of one who is learned in his own special line.

And such is the behavior of the specialist. He will take a position — in politics, in art, in social matters, in the other sciences — and it will be that of a primitive, of an ignoramus. And he will take these positions forcefully and with self-assurance, without allowing — and this is the paradox — for specialists in those other fields. On making this type of man into a specialist, civilization has made him hermetic and self-satisfied within his own limitations. And this self-assurance of his own worth and importance leads him to set himself up as an authority outside his specialty. So that even though he represents the maximum of qualification — in his specialty — and therefore the quality most opposed to mass-man, he will act as someone without qualifications, as a mass-man, in almost all other spheres of life.

This is not a vague observation. Anyone who cares to do so can observe the stupidity with which our "men of science" think, judge, and act today in the fields of politics, art, religion, and as regards the general problems of life and the world. The other specialists — doctors, engineers, financiers, professors, and so on — are just as bad. The state of "not listening," of not deferring to higher knowledge, with which we have repeatedly characterized mass-man, reaches its climax in these partially qualified specialists. They symbolize and in large part constitute the present imperium of the mass-man, and their barbarism is the most immediate cause of the demoralization of Europe.

Furthermore, they are the best example of how the civilization of the last century, *left to its own devices and inclinations,* has produced this resurgence of primitivism and barbarism.

The most immediate result of this *unbalanced* specialization has been that today, when there are more "men of science" than ever, there are fewer "cultured" men than there were, say, in 1750. And the worst of it is that these scientific worker-bees do not even ensure the inner progress of science. For science from time to time requires, for the organic regulation of its own advance, an effort at reconstitution, something which becomes more and more difficult as it involves ever-wider regions of knowledge. Newton was able to create his system of physics without knowing much philosophy, but Einstein needed to immerse himself in Kant and Mach before he could achieve his own keen synthesis. Kant and Mach: the names are mere symbols of the enormous mass of philosophical and psychological thought which impinged on Einstein, and they served to *liberate* his mind and to clear the way for his innovations. Yet Einstein is not enough. Physics is entering on the most profound crisis in its history, and it can be saved only by a new *Encyclopedia* more systematic than the French original.

The specialization which made possible the progress of experimental science for a century is approaching a stage where it can no longer continue its advance on its own, unless a better generation provides it with a new form of prime mover.

But if the specialist is ignorant of the basic philosophy of the science he cultivates, he is more profoundly ignorant of the historical conditions requisite for its existence and continuation, that is, of how society and the mind of man must be disposed so that there may continue to be researchers. The notable decrease of vocations in pure science is a disquieting symptom for anyone with a clear idea of what constitutes civilization, an idea usually lacking in the typical "man of science," the shining exemplar of our culture. He, like the mass-man, believes that civilization is simply *out there* — in the same way as the earth's crust and the primitive jungle.

13

The Greatest Danger: The State

IN ANY RIGHT ordering of public affairs, the mass is the part
which does not act on its own. That is its mission. It has
come into the world to be directed, influenced, represented,
organized—even to the point of ceasing to be a mass, or at
least of aspiring to this possibility. But it has not come into
the world to do anything by itself. It needs to have recourse
to higher authority, to appeal to selected minorities. Who
these minorities may be can be argued endlessly, but, whether
they be one set of men or another, humanity could not exist
in its essentials without this condition of subordination. It
would be prudent to recognize this truth, though the world
spend another century with its head hidden, ostrich-fashion,
to avoid seeing something that is altogether obvious. For it
is not a matter of an opinion based on facts more or less frequent and probable, but on a law of "social physics," much
more immutable than the laws of Newton's physics. The day
when an authentic philosophy* once more predominates in
Europe—and that is the only thing that can save it—it will
once again be recognized that man is, whether he likes it or

* For philosophy to rule, it is not necessary that philosophers be
rulers (as Plato at first wanted) nor even that rulers philosophize (as
he more modestly wished later). Both courses would prove fatal.
For philosophy to rule it suffices that it exist, that is, that philosophers be philosophers. For over a century now philosophers have
been everything but philosophers: they have been politicians, ped-
agogues, professors, men of letters, and men of science.

not, a being forced by his nature to seek some higher authority. If he succeeds in finding a higher authority by himself,
he is a superior man. If not, he is a mass-man and must
receive it from his natural superiors.

For the mass to claim the right to act on its own is, then,
to rebel against its own destiny, and, since that is what it is
doing now, we here speak of the rebellion of the masses. For
in the end, the only thing that can truly and properly be called
rebellion is that which consists in not accepting one's own
destiny, in rebelling against oneself. The rebelliousness of
the Archangel Lucifer would not have been any the less if, instead of insisting on being God, which was not his destiny,
he had insisted on being the least of the angels, which was
also not his destiny. (If Lucifer had been a Russian, like Tolstoy,
he might perhaps have preferred the latter form of rebellion,
which goes against God neither less nor more than the famous
revolt itself.)

Whenever the mass acts on its own, it does so in only one
manner, for it has no other: in effect it carries out a lynching.
It is not entirely by chance that lynch law comes from America, for America is, in its own fashion, the paradise of the
masses. It is even less surprising that now, when the masses
are in the ascendant, violence is also in the ascendant and is
made the ultimate *ratio*, the final reason, the only doctrine.
For some time now, the process of violence has become the
norm.* Nowadays it has reached its height of development,
and that can be a good symptom, for it means that its decline
is at hand. Violence is now the rhetoric of the day: inane
dogmatic rhetoricians have made it their own. When a human reality has run its course, completed its history, when it
has been lost and cast away, the waves throw it up on the
shore, on the rocks of rhetoric, and there, although already
a corpse, it remains for some time. Rhetoric is the cemetery
of realities. At best, it is a hospital. A dead reality is survived

* See *España invertebrada*, First edition, 1921.

by its name, which though it is only a word, preserves some of a word's magic power.

Even though the prestige of violence as a cynically established norm may have begun to diminish, we shall continue to live under its rule, though it be under another form.

I refer to the gravest danger now threatening Western civilization. Like all the other dangers which menace it, this one is a creature of civilization itself, one of its glories, in fact: the modern state. We find here a replica of the situation confronting science: the fertility of its principles impels it toward fabulous progress, but this progress inexorably imposes upon it a specialization which threatens to strangle it.

The same process holds true for the state.

We need only recall what the state was in all European nations at the end of the eighteenth century. Quite a small affair! Early capitalism and its industrial organization, in which the new, rationalized technology had triumphed, brought about an initial expansion of society. A new social class appeared, more powerful in number and potential than any one previously: the middle class. This fractious middle class possessed one quality above and before all else: a talent for the practical. It knew how to organize, impose discipline, lend continuity and consistency to its endeavors. In the midst of all this, as on an ocean, the "Ship of State" sailed along on its perilous course. The "Ship of State" is a metaphor reinvented by the bourgeoisie, which felt itself to be oceanic, omnipotent—and impervious to storms. At the time, that ship was a small craft: it carried few marines, a scant officialdom, and had a small payroll. It had been built in the Middle Ages by a class of men very different from any middle class: by the nobles, admirable for their courage and their talent for command, and for their sense of responsibility. Without them, the nations of Europe would not now exist. With all their virtues, virtues of the heart and gut, the nobility, then and now, have second-rate minds. They acted from the viscera, from their gut-feelings. Of limited intelligence, sentimental, even maudlin, they were instinctive, intuitive, in short "irrational." Hence they were unable to develop technology, a process which requires thought, rationalization. For instance, they failed to invent the gunpowder on which military power depended, and they were bested. Incapable of inventing new arms, they allowed the emerging bourgeoisie, who traded with the Orient or wherever, to introduce and utilize gunpowder and weaponry. Thus the defeat of the noble warrior, the gentleman on horseback, the knight so iron-clad he could scarcely move in battle. It had never occurred to this noble warrior that the eternal secret of warfare does not consist so much in defense as in offense, a secret which was to be rediscovered by Napoleon.*

Inasmuch as the state is a matter of technique — of public order and administration — the older order, the *ancien régime*, reaches the end of the eighteenth century with a very weak state, harassed on all sides by widespread social revolt. The disproportion between the power of society and that of the state at that time, as compared to their relative proportion at the time of Charlemagne, makes the eighteenth century state look degenerate. The Carolingian state was much less power-

* This simple image of the great historic change in which the supremacy of the nobles was replaced by the predominance of the bourgeois was first given us by Ranke [Leopold von Ranke, 1795-1886, the German historian]. Obviously this schematic, symbolic truth requires much supplementation to make it more complete. Gunpowder has been known from time immemorial. Putting a charge of it into a tube was developed by a man in Lombardy. Even then, it was not efficacious until the invention of the cast cannonball. The nobles used firearms to a limited extent, but it proved too costly. It was not until the time of bourgeois armies, better organized financially, that it could be widely used. Strictly speaking, the nobles, represented by the medieval type army of the Burgundians, were definitively defeated by the new nonprofessional bourgeois army formed by the Swiss, whose primary force lay in the new discipline and the new rationalization of tactics.

ful than that of Louis XVI, but then of course the society around it had no power whatever.* The disproportion in the eighteenth century made possible the revolution: the French Revolution and others up until 1848.

Following the French Revolution, the middle class took over public power and applied its own undeniable virtues to the state. In little more than a generation the bourgeoisie created a powerful state, which put an end to revolution. Since 1848, that is, from the time of the second generation of bourgeois government, there has not been a real revolution in Europe. Not because there have not been motives for one, but because the means have been missing. Public power was brought up to the level of social power. *Goodbye forever to Revolution!* Now, in the West, only its opposite is possible: the coup d'etat. Everything that gave itself the airs of a revolution in subsequent years was no more than a coup d'etat in disguise.

In our time the state has become a formidable machine which functions wondrously because of the quantity and precision of its means. Implanted in the midst of society, the state need only press a button to set in motion its enormous levers and bring its overwhelming power to act in a decisive manner on any part of the social body.

* It would be well to emphasize this point, and to make clear that the epoch of the absolute monarchies in Europe coincided with very weak states. How is this to be explained? Society around them had begun to grow. But why, if the state was all-powerful — it *was* "absolute" — did it not ensure its strength and make itself stronger? We have already alluded to one of the reasons: the incapacity of the blood aristocracies for technical, rationalized, bureaucratic organization. But this explanation is not sufficient. It also happens that in the absolute state *those aristocracies did not wish to aggrandize the state at the expense of society as a whole.* Contrary to common belief, the absolute state instinctively respects society in general to a greater degree than our democratic state, which, though more intelligent, shows less sense of historical responsibility.

The contemporary state is the most visible and striking product of civilization. It is an interesting revelation to note the attitude adopted toward it by the mass-man. He can see it, admire it, know *it is there*, safeguarding his existence; but he has no notion that it is a creation of human beings, invented by certain men and maintained by certain virtues and presuppositions which were held by men in the past, but could disappear tomorrow. Moreover, the mass-man sees in the state an anonymous power, and since he feels himself to be anonymous too, he believes that the state is something of his own. When conflict or crisis occurs in public life, the mass-man will tend to look to the state to assume the burden, take on the problem, take charge directly of solving the matter with its unsurpassable means.

And this is the greatest danger threatening civilization today: the statification of life, state intervention, the taking over by the state of all social spontaneity. And this amounts to the annulment of historical spontaneity, which is what sustains, nourishes, and impels all human destiny. Whenever the mass suspects some misfortune, or when it is moved by its prurient appetite, the temptation is there to look to the permanent and secure possibility of getting everything — without effort, argument, doubt, or risk — to call on this marvellous machinery which goes into action with the touch of a button. The mass tells itself: "The state is me," its own version of *L'État, c'est moi*. And that is a complete mistake. The state is the mass only in the same sense that two men can say they are identical merely because neither of them is called John. The contemporary state and the mass are the same only in being anonymous. But the mass-man nevertheless believes that he is the state, and he will increasingly tend to want it to be set in motion on the least pretext, to crush any creative minority which disturbs it, disturbs it in any way whatsoever: in politics, ideas, industry.

The result of this tendency will prove fatal. Social spontaneity will be constantly violated by state intervention; no new seeds will bear fruit. Society will have to live *for* the state, man *for* the governmental machine. And inasmuch as the state is only a machine whose existence and maintenance depend on the vital support given it, it will, after having sucked out the marrow of society, be itself left bloodless, reduced to a skeleton, and will meet the death of rusted machinery, a grimmer death than that endured by a living organism.

Such was the sorry fate of ancient civilization. The imperial state created by the Julii and the Claudii was doubtless an admirable machine, incomparably superior as artifact to the old republican state created by the patrician families. But curiously enough, it had scarcely reached maturity when the body politic began to decline. Already in the time of the Antonines (second century) the unnatural supremacy of the state had begun to weigh down society. The latter became enslaved, unable to live except *in the service of the state*. Life as a whole was bureaucratized. What happened? The bureaucratization of life brought about its total decay in all strata. Wealth diminished, women became less fruitful. In order to cover its own needs, the state enforced a growing bureaucratization of human existence. This tightening of the screws amounted to a militarization of society. The major priority of the state became its war apparatus, the army. The state became before all else the producer of security (the same security, be it remembered, out of which the mass-man was born). Hence, an army was the first prerequisite. The Severi, of African origin, militarized the world. A vain undertaking! The wretchedness continued, wombs grew increasingly barren, even soldiers could not be found. After the Severi, the army had to be recruited among foreigners.

Is the paradoxical, tragic process of statism not clear? In order that society at large can live better it creates the state as instrument. And then the state takes over, and society must begin to live for the state. In the end, however, even the state is made up of people from that society. But soon these people are not enough to maintain it and foreigners must be called in: first the Dalmatians, then the Germans. These foreigners take over the state, and the rest of society, the original populace, must live as slaves to them, to people altogether alien, people with whom they have nothing in common.* This is where state intervention has led them: the populace is converted into fuel for the state machine, which was originally a mere artifact. The skeleton wears away the flesh around it. The scaffolding becomes tenant and landlord of the house.

When one knows all this, it is astonishing to hear how Mussolini heralded, with his matchless petulance, a prodigious new discovery, made in Italy, enunciated in a formula: "Everything for the State. Nothing outside the State. Nothing against the State." This formula-statement alone would suffice to reveal that fascism was a movement typical of mass-man. On coming to power, Mussolini found himself with a state admirably constructed—not by him, of course, but by the very forces and ideas he opposed: those of liberal democracy. He simply used the state ruthlessly. The results of his work cannot be compared in point of worth to those obtained by the political and administrative functioning of the liberal state. If he achieved anything at all, it was so minute, so invisible, and of so little substance that it did not justify the accumulation of abnormal power which allowed him to use the state's machinery in an extreme form.

Statism is a high form of violence and of direct action so constituted as to be the norm. Through and by means of the state—that anonymous machine—the masses act for themselves.

The nations of Europe face great internal difficulties of every kind, problems of law, economics, and public order. Are we not justified in fearing that under the dominion of the masses the state may well endeavor to crush the in-

---

* Remember the last words spoken by Lucius Septimius Severus to his sons: *Stay together, pay the soldiers, and ignore the rest.*

dependence of the individual and the small group, and thus once and for all obliterate the hopes of the future?

A concrete example of the state mechanism is to be found in one of the most alarming phenomena of recent years: the enormous increase of the police forces in all countries. The increase in population has made this process inevitable. However accustomed we may be to it, it is a terrible paradox that in a modern city the constant movement of people going about their affairs requires a vast police force merely to regulate traffic. But it is naive for people who believe in law and order to think that these forces of public order will always be content to impose the kind of order the citizens want. It is almost inevitable that the forces of order will define and decide what kind of order they are going to impose, and in the end it may well be the kind of order which suits them best.

Now that we have touched on the matter, we would do well to note the different reactions of two societies to the public need for order. About 1800, when the new industrial development began to create the industrial worker, a type of man more given to crime than traditional man, France reacted by creating a larger police force. In 1810 similar causes led to an increase of crime in England, and the English suddenly found they had no police. The Conservatives were in power. What would they do? Would they create a new police force? Nothing of the kind. They preferred to put up with crime to the limit of their endurance. "The public was prepared, if necessary, to put up with a certain amount of disorder, if it was the price of freedom. 'They have an admirable police at Paris,' wrote John William Ward, 'but they pay for it dear enough. I had rather half-a-dozen people's throats should be cut in Ratcliffe Highway every three or four years than be subject to domiciliary visits, spies, and all the rest of Fouché's contrivances.' "[1] Here we have two different views on the state. The English Conservative of the time wanted the state to have limits.

Part II
WHO RULES THE WORLD?

14

Who Rules the World?

WESTERN CIVILIZATION ITSELF, as we have repeatedly shown, has inevitably brought about the rebellion of the masses. From a certain point of view this development presents a favorable aspect: for as we have also pointed out, the rebellion of the masses is one and the same thing as the fabulous increase in the standard of living in modern times. But the reverse side of this phenomenon is fearsome: the rebellion of the masses represents a radical demoralization of humanity. Let us consider the matter from new points of view.

I

The substance or character of any new historical period is the result of internal variations in man or spirit, or the result of external—formal, mechanical as it were—variations. Among the latter, the most important, surely, is a displacement in power; but this entails a displacement in spirit as well.

Consequently, when we set about examining a period with a view to understanding it, one of our first questions ought to be: who rules the world? It may be that at the time in question, humanity is scattered in varied ways, without communication between the segments, so that they form internal, independent worlds. In the days of Miltiades, the Mediterranean world was unaware of the existence of the Far-Eastern world. In such cases we would have to consider the question in relation to each world. But beginning with the sixteenth century the whole of humanity has entered upon a

vast process of unification which in our times has reached its
farthest limit. No significant portion of humanity now lives
apart: there are no islands of humanity any more. In consequence, since the sixteenth century, it can truly be said that
whoever rules in the world does, in effect, exert an author-
itative influence over the whole of it. Such has been the role
of the homogeneous group formed by European peoples during the past three centuries and more. Europe ruled, and,
under its aegis the world lived in a unitary mode, or at least
was progressively unified.

This style of life is commonly known as the "Modern Age,"
a colorless inexpressive name which conceals the basic reality:
it was the epoch of European hegemony.

By "rule" we need not understand primarily the exercise of
material power, of physical coercion. We are trying to avoid
foolish terms, at least the more gross and obvious ones. Now:
the normal, stable relation between men for which we have
used the term "rule" *never rests on force*; on the contrary, it
is precisely because a man or a group of men exercises command that he or they have at their disposition the social apparatus or machine known as "force." Those cases in which
at first glance rule seems to have been based on force are
revealed on closer inspection as the best examples of our
thesis. Napoleon mounted an undisguised aggression against
Spain, maintained his campaign for some time, but never
"ruled" Spain for a single day. And this was so although he
had force, or more precisely because all he had was force. We
must distinguish between an act or process of aggression and
the condition of ruling. Rule is the normal exercise of authority, and it is always based on public opinion, the same today
as it was ten thousand years ago, whether among the civilized
English or the Bushmen. No one has ever ruled on earth on
the basis of anything other than public opinion.

Or does anyone think that the sovereignty of public opinion is an invention of the lawyer Danton in 1789 or by St.
Thomas Aquinas in the thirteenth century? The notion of

this sovereignty may have been discovered in one place or another, at one time or another, but the fact that public opinion is the root force which produces the phenomenon of rule in human societies is as old and perennial as man himself. In Newton's physics, gravitation is the force which produces movement. And the force which is public opinion is the law of universal gravitation in political history. Without it the science of history itself would be impossible. Hence, Hume's acute observation that the theme of history consists in demonstrating how the sovereignty of public opinion, far from being an utopian aspiration, always constitutes the weight that has counted at all times in human society. Even the man who tries to rule with the help of mercenaries is dependent on their opinion and on the opinion of them held by the rest of the population.

The truth is that no one rules with mercenaries. As Talleyrand said to Napoleon: "You can do everything with bayonets, Sire, except sit on them." And ruling is not a matter of seizing power, but the easy exercise of it. In sum, to rule is to sit down, be it on a throne, curule chair, front bench, ministerial seat, or bishop's cathedra. Contrary to the naive melodramatic view, ruling is not so much a question of a heavy hand as a firm seat. The state is, in effect, the state of opinion. It is a position of equilibrium, a balance of pressures.

At times public opinion does not exist, however. A society divided into discordant groups, the force of whose opinion reciprocally cancels each other out, leaves no room for a ruling power to be constituted. And, inasmuch as nature abhors a vacuum, the void left by the absence of the force of public opinion is filled with brute force. At most then, brute force is a substitute for public opinion.

Thus, the law of public opinion is the law of historical gravitation. But to be exact, we must take into consideration the times when public opinion is absent. Then, we arrive at a formula which is a well-known, venerable, and forthright commonplace: no one can be said to "rule" against public opinion.

This leads us to the realization that "to rule" signifies the preponderance of an opinion, and therefore of a spirit; that therefore ruling is, in the end, a matter of spiritual power. The evidence of history meticulously confirms this view. All primitive rule possesses a "sacred" character; it is founded on religion, and religion is the first form taken by what is called spirit, idea, opinion: in sum, it is founded on the immaterial and ultraphysical. In the Middle Ages the same phenomenon is seen in a larger format. The first state or public authority formed in Europe is the church, with its particular and well-defined character as "spiritual power." From the church the political power learned that it, too, was originally a spiritual authority, and thus it created the *Holy* Roman Empire. Thus there is rivalry between two equally spiritual powers; but they do not find any substantive differences, for they are both spirit, and they arrive at an agreement each to exert hegemony over one of the two time modes, the temporal and the eternal. Temporal power and spiritual power are identically spiritual, but one represents the spirit of the time (intramundane and ephemeral public opinion) while the other represents the spirit of eternity (God's opinion rather than that of the public, God's view of man and his destiny).

To say that at a given period such and such a man, people, or homogeneous group of peoples *rules* is the same as saying that such and such a system of opinions — ideas, preferences, aspirations, purposes — is dominant.

How are we to understand this predominance? Most human beings have no opinions of their own. These must be supplied from outside like pressurized lubricants for a machine. Some spirit, some spiritual force or other, must hold authority and exercise it, so that people who have no opinion — and they are the majority — can embrace a position. Without the existence of opinions, human coexistence would be reduced to chaos; even worse, to historical nullity; the life of mankind would be lacking in architecture, in organic order. Without a spiritual authority, *without someone to command,* and in the measure that this lack is felt, chaos prevails. Similarly, *all displacement of power,* all change of authority, is at the same time a shift in opinion, and therefore nothing less than a change of historical gravitation.

Let us now return to the beginning. For several centuries Europe ruled the world, and Europe was a conglomerate of peoples spiritually akin. During the Middle Ages there was no such authority in temporal matters. Such has been the case in all of history's middle ages. That is why they are times of relative chaos and relative barbarism, representing a deficit in opinion. They are times in which men and women love, hate, desire, detest, all without limit — but there is a dearth of opinion. Such times are not lacking in charm and delight. But in great epochs mankind thrives on opinion and, therefore, order rules. On the other side of the Middle Ages, we find an epoch in which, as in the Modern Age, someone is in command, though only in a certain enclosed portion of the world: Rome, the great directress. She brought order to the Mediterranean and around its shores.

Following our wars, Europe and its civilization are no longer said to be dominant in the world. Little thought is devoted to the implications. The diagnosis implies a displacement of power and authority. Whither is it shifting? Who will succeed Europe in dominance? Is it certain that anyone will take its place? And if no one can, what is going to happen?

II

The truth is that there occurs at every instant, and therefore right now, an infinitude of things. Any attempt to say what is really happening right now must be understood as something of an irony. But for the very reason that we are unable to have direct and complete knowledge of reality, we have no alternative but arbitrarily to construct some reality, to suppose that things are happening in a certain fashion.

This supposition will provide us with a scheme, that is, a concept or a congeries of concepts. We can then look at reality, as a navigator with his quadrant, and obtain an approximate projection. The scientific method and the use of the intellect as a whole depends on such projection and approximation. When we see a friend coming up the garden path and say "Here's Peter," we are deliberately, and ironically, committing an error. For us, "Peter" signifies a schematic repertory of physical and moral behavior, what we may call "character," and the truth is that our friend Peter sometimes is not at all like the concept "our friend Peter."

Every concept, the most ordinary as well as the most technical, is mounted in the setting of its own irony, like a set of teeth in a halcyonic grin, or a square-cut diamond set in gold. The concept seriously claims that "this thing is A, this B." But the seriousness is that of a *pince-nez* on a sly joker: it is the equivocal humor of a man suppressing a laugh, who, unless he purses his lips, will burst out in a guffaw. The concept and the man know very well that A is not A just like that, nor is B ever simply B. There is more to it than what is said, and in that duplicity lies the irony. What is really to be understood by the concept and by its enunciator is, in effect, that "I know very well that this thing is not A nor is that thing B; but by taking them to be such, I come to an understanding with myself for practical purposes and for adopting a viable attitude toward both cases."

This theory of rational knowledge would have displeased the Greek of classic times. For the Greek thought he had discovered in reason, in the concept, reality itself. We, on the other hand, believe that reason, that is, the concept, is one of man's household utensils, something he needs and uses to clarify his own position in the midst of the infinite and highly problematic reality which constitutes his life. Life is a struggle with things so as to maintain oneself among them. Concepts are the strategic plan which we form to maintain ourselves, to defend ourselves in the battle. And thus we find, if we plumb the depths of any concept, that it tells us nothing about the thing itself, but rather sums up how we can act or be acted upon. This circumstantial view, this opinion which holds that the content of a concept is always vital, embodying a possible activity or a possible passivity, a possible endurance if nothing more, has not ever before been sustained by anyone, so far as I know. Nevertheless, it is the inevitable outcome of the philosophic process intitiated by Kant. For if we reassess philosophy up to the time of Kant in this light, we may be struck by the fact that *fundamentally* all philosophers have repeated each other. Every philosophical discovery is no more than an un-covery, an uncovering and bringing to the surface of what was lying in the depths.

But this has become an inordinate introduction to what I am about to say, which is, moreover, something quite apart from philosophic problems. I was simply going to point out that what is really happening in the world—the world of history, be it understood—is no more than the following: for three centuries Europe ruled the world and now Europe is no longer sure of what it is. Of course, I exaggerate: to reduce to such simple terms the infinitude of factors which make up the present historic reality is doubtless and at best a pure exaggeration. But I am forced to remember that to think is to exaggerate, whether one wants to or not. Whoever prefers not to exaggerate had best remain silent; or worse, paralyze his intellect, and find the best way to act the idiot.

I believe, in short, that the aforementioned trend is the key happening in the world, and that all the rest is merely a consequence, condition, symptom, or incident of this larger fact.

I have not maintained that Europe and the West have ceased to rule in effect, but only that the West is beset with grave doubts as to whether it continues to exert hegemony or will do so tomorrow. In the rest of the world there is a congruent sentiment: they wonder if they are now ruled by anyone at all. They are not sure.

Throughout this century much has been said and written about the decadence of Europe and the decline of the West. I would ask people not to think automatically of Oswald Spengler whenever the decline of the West is mentioned. Before his famous book appeared, everyone was talking about the phenomenon, and the success of his book, as is well known, is due to the fact that for the most heterogeneous reasons people felt with their senses that the decline was manifest, or had a suspicion that such was the case.

There has been so much talk of decadence and decline that many have taken it to be a *fait accompli*, a thoroughly accomplished fact. Not that they are entirely serious, I am sure, or have overwhelming proof, but rather because they have been habituated to the idea, even if they cannot recall the exact date of their conversion. Waldo Frank's *The Re-discovery of America*[1] was entirely based on the supposition that Europe is in its death-throes. And yet Frank neither analyzes nor directly discusses, or even questions, such an enormous supposition, one that is to serve him as a formidable premise. Without adducing proof, he sets off from this premise as if from something incontrovertible. The ingenuousness he displays from the outset suffices to show that Frank was scarcely sure of the decadence of Europe. Far from it: he never even put the question, never asked himself about his presupposition. He takes it as he would take a bus. Commonplaces are the autobuses of intellectual transport.

And as he did, so do many others. Even worse, so do societies, entire nations.

The world at present is offering a perfect spectacle of puerility. When someone passes the word in school that the teacher has gone, the child-mob is apt to run wild. They are freed from the pressure imposed by the teacher, free to throw off the yoke and kick over the traces, free to kick up their heels, to stand on their heads and to feel themselves masters of their own fate. But once the rules which organized their lives, tasks, and occupations are taken away, the child-mob finds it has no real occupation of its own, no formal task, no goal with any sense, continuity, or point to it, so there is only one thing left to do — stand on its head.

The lesser nations of the world today offer an even more frivolous and deplorable spectacle than the world at large. Since Europe is said to be in decline, and is therefore no longer in a position to exercise hegemony, every half-baked brand-new nation[2] begins to kick up its heels, make wild gestures, and stand on its head, or it struts like a rooster giving itself the airs of total command of its own fate. Hence, the shaky view of nationalism that one encounters on all sides.

In previous chapters we have attempted to classify the new type of man who predominates in the world: we have called him mass-man and have noted that the principal characteristic of this "common man" consists in demanding the right to be as common as he is and wants to be and in refusing to accept any authority higher than his own. It was only natural that if this mentality is predominant among every people, it should occur among nations as well. There are also mass-people bent on rebellion against the great creative peoples or nations who are the minority stock and who have created history. It is a truly comic sight to see some brat of a republic standing on its toes in some out-of-the-way lost corner of the globe to denounce Europe and read it out of universal history.

What are the results? Europe created a system of standards whose efficacy and productiveness the centuries confirmed. Those standards are not — far from it — the best possible. But they are definitive, so long as better ones do not exist or are not in sight. Before supplanting them, others must be engendered. Now, the mass-peoples have resolved to declare civilized European standards bankrupt. But, since they are incapable of creating others, they know not what to do, and to fill in — they stand on their heads.

Such is the first consequence which follows when there is no one left in the world to rule. Those in rebellion are left without a meaningful task to perform, without a program for life.

III

The story goes that when the gypsy went to confession, the priest guardedly asked him if he knew the commandments of God's law. The gypsy answered: "Look, Father, I *was* going to learn them, but I heard they were about to do away with them."

Is this not the situation in the world today? A rumor is circulating to the effect that the commandments of the law of Europe are about to be done away with, that they are no longer in force. And so, men and nations take the occasion and opportunity to live without imperatives. For the only imperatives that existed were European. It is not a question of new standards arising to replace the old ones, as has happened in the past, or of brand-new fervor's youthful fire reviving old enthusiasms which have grown cold. That would be a natural development. Now, the old *is* said to be old, not because it is senile, but because it is confronted with a new principle, which has an immediate advantage over the old simply because it is new. By the same token, if we had no children, we would not seem quite so old, or it would seem to take longer to get old. And the same thing happens with artifacts or machines. An automobile ten years old seems older than a locomotive twenty years old simply because inventions in the automotive industry have followed each other with greater rapidity. This kind of "decadence," then, which originates in the burgeoning of the new, of youth, is altogether normal, a symptom of good health.

But what is taking place in Europe today is unhealthy, unsound. The European commandments have lost their force, while there are no new ones to be seen on the horizon. Europe, it is claimed, has ceased to rule, and there is no one in sight to take over. By Europe we mean, primarily, the trinity of France, England, and Germany. The body of norms for human existence according to which the civilized world has been formed and has matured were developed in those portions of the globe which these nations occupy. If, as is now claimed, these three nations are in decadence and their program of life has lost its worth, then it is no wonder the world is demoralized.

And that is the simple truth. The whole world—nations and individuals—is demoralized. For a while, decadence is amusing and even vaguely spirited. Lesser people feel that a weight has been lifted from them. Ever since they were written on stone or bronze, the decalogues retain their weighty character. The etymology of "to command" implies "to load," to put something in someone's hands. Whoever commands is, perforce, a person who loads one down. At this juncture the lesser people of the world are tired of being loaded down, of being burdened with anything, and they now take advantage of being exonerated from weighty imperatives, and do so with a certain festive air. But the *fiesta* is short lived. Without commandments obliging us to live in certain fashions, our lives become purely arbitrary, they become "expendable." This is the terrible spiritual dilemma in which the world's best youth find themselves today. By dint of feeling themselves "free," exempt from restrictions, they feel empty. A life which is "expendable" is a greater negation of existence than death. To live is to have something definite to do, a mission to fulfill, and in the measure that we avoid dedicating our life to something we empty our life of meaning. Soon a cry will go up from around the planet, rising like the howl of an innumerable pack of wild dogs baying at the stars, crying for someone or something to take command and impose a mission.

So much for those who proclaim, with childish innocence, that Europe has ceased to exercise a dominant influence. To command means to supply people with a mission, to give them their bearings, to allot them a destiny. It is also to impede their extravagance, which tends to be a mere wandering aimlessly through a vague and desolate emptiness.

It would make little difference if Europe ceased to exert its authority as the dominant culture if there were an alternative in sight. But there is not a shadow of a substitute. New York and Moscow represent nothing new relative to Europe. They are both segments of the European order; in disassociating themselves from the rest of Europe they lose part of their meaning. In plain truth, it is disconcerting to speak of New York and Moscow. For one does not know for sure what they really are: the decisive word has not been said of either of them yet. Still, one has an idea of their generic character. Both qualify fully to be included in what I have sometimes called "the phenomenon of historical camouflage." By nature camouflage is a reality which is not what it seems to be. Its appearance conceals its substance instead of declaring it. Naturally, most people are deceived. Only those who know beforehand that camouflage is involved avoid the deception. It is the same as with a mirage. Our preconception alters our vision.

In every instance of historical camouflage two realities are to be found: the one, substantive, effectual, deep-seated; the other, apparent, accidental, superficial. Thus, in Moscow we find a layer or film of European ideas — Marxism — thought out in Europe in terms of European realities and problems. Beneath this surface screen there is a people not only ethnically different from Europeans, but also — and this is far more important — living in an age different from ours. That people is still in ferment: in short, they are in an earlier age, they are a child-people. For Marxism to have triumphed in Russia — where there was no industry — would have been the greatest contradiction which could have befallen Marxism. But no such contradiction exists for there was no such triumph. Russia is Marxist in approximately the same measure the Germans in the Holy Roman Empire were Romans. New people do not have *ideas*. When they grow up in an ambience where an ancient culture still exists or recently existed, they cloak themselves in that culture's ideas. This is their camouflage.

It is often forgotten that there are two types of evolution

for any people. There is the people which is born into a "world" devoid of civilization, as were, for example, the Egyptians or the Chinese. Everything such a people does is autochthonous, and their acts are obvious, with a direct sense of their own. But there are other people who germinate and develop in an ambience steeped in venerable history. Only consider Rome, which developed in the Mediterranean world, on a sea whose shores were rich in Graeco-Oriental culture. Naturally, a half of Roman ways were ones they had learned rather than invented. A way of behaving which has been handed down has a double aspect, a meaning which is not direct, but oblique. Whoever does something he has learned — even using a word from a foreign language — is making an authentic gesture of his own: for instance, translating the foreign term into his own language. And so, to understand about camouflage it is necessary to look at it obliquely, to look at it in the way one translates a foreign text with a dictionary at hand. I await the appearance of a book in which Stalinist Marxism is translated into the history of Russia. For Russia's strength lies in what is Russian and not in what is Communist. Who knows what it will become! The only certainty is that Russia will need centuries to *take up hegemony*. Because it still lacks norms for rule, commandments, it has had to feign adherence to the European principles of Marx. Since it is youthful, overendowed with youth, this piece of fiction suited. Youth does not need reasons to live; pretexts suffice.

Something of the same sort is true as regards New York. To attribute its strength to the precepts it follows is also an error in this case as well. In the final analysis these precepts can be reduced to one: technology or technicism. And how odd! For that is another European invention, not an American one. Technology was invented in Europe in the eighteenth and nineteenth centuries. How odd again! For these are the very centuries in which America was coming into being. And we are seriously told that the essence of America is its concept of practicality and technique, instead of being told that America is, like all colonies everywhere, a rejuvenation of ancient races, especially of those from Europe. For reasons different from those in the case of Russia, the United States also represents an example of that specific historical reality we call "a new people." This description is often considered as merely a phrase, when in fact it is as effective and precise as the use of the word "youth," when applied to a man. America is strong because of its youth, which it has placed at the service of the contemporary commandment of technology—of "technique"—just as it might have placed it at the service of Buddhism, if that were the order of the day. But in doing as it does, America has only begun its history. It is only now that its trials and tribulations, its dissensions and conflicts are beginning. It has much to do, some of it completely the opposite of the technical and practical. America is even younger than Russia. I have always maintained, though fearful of possible exaggeration, that the Americans are a primitive people camouflaged in the latest inventions.* In his *Re-discovery of America*, Waldo Frank declares it openly. America has not yet truly suffered. It is illusory to think that this people could possess the virtues of command.

To avoid the pessimistic conclusion that nobody is going to exercise sovereignty and that, therefore, the historical world must fall back into chaos, we will have to return to the point whence we started and ask seriously: Is it so certain that Europe is in decline, as decadent as people say, and that it has abdicated, resigned its dominance? May not this apparent decline be a fortunate crisis which will allow Europe to be itself, literally to be Europe? Was not the decline of the *nations* of Europe an a priori necessity for the eventual formation of a United States of Europe, for the plurality of Europe to be replaced by its formal unity?

* See the essay "Hegel y América" in *El Espectador*, VII, 1930.

IV

The functions of commanding and of obeying are decisive in any society. So long as there is any doubt as to who commands and who obeys, everything else will be in a muddle, deficient and ineffective. Even the innermost consciousness of individuals, with a few outstanding exceptions, will be falsified and in disarray. If man were a solitary being, finding himself thrown into contact and association with others only on occasion, he might remain intact after such encounters, remaining himself despite the repercussions from displacements and strains in the ruling power. But inasmuch as he is a social being to his marrow, his private being is disarranged by changes which strictly speaking directly affect the collectivity only. Hence, if an individual be scrutinized on his own, it is possible to determine without further data the state of his country's conscience in the matter of command and obedience.

It would be interesting, and perhaps useful, to look at the individual character of the average Spaniard, which is the one I know best. It would be depressing, however, and I do not care to delve too deeply there. And yet it would serve to show the great degree of personal demoralization, of degradation, produced in such a man as a result of Spain's being a nation which for centuries has lived with a false conscience as regards the hierarchy of command. This degradation merely follows from the acceptance of misgovernment as a constituted norm even though it continues to be felt as wrong. Inasmuch as what is essentially abnormal and criminal cannot be converted into a sound norm, the individual chooses to adapt himself to the abnormality by making himself a homogeneous part of the crime weighing upon him. The mechanism is similar to that which gives rise to the popular saying "One lie breeds a hundred." All nations have passed through periods in which those who have no right to rule have insisted on doing so; but a strong instinct to resist has prevailed, and eventually a nation's energy is concentrated on expelling the pretenders to power. Such nations have rejected this transitory irregularity and thus reconstituted their morale as a people. But the Spanish have done the opposite: instead of resisting a form of authority which their consciences rejected, they have preferred to falsify their natures in every way so as to accommodate themselves to the initial fraud. While such an attitude prevails it is useless to expect anything of worth. Any society whose state and authority is by nature fraudulent is incapable of the expansive vigor needed to properly maintain a place in history.

There is, then, nothing strange in the fact that any doubt or hesitation as to who is exercising sovereignty and authority in the world is enough to bring about the beginnings of total demoralization in public life, and in private lives as well.

By its very nature, human life must be dedicated to something, an enterprise glorious or humble, a destiny illustrious or modest. This is a condition strange but inexorable, inseparable from our very existence. On the one hand, to live is something each one does for and by himself. On the other, if this life of mine, which only matters to me, is not dedicated by me to something, it will go along in a loose disjointed way, lacking the necessary tension and "form." In these years we are witnesses to the immense spectacle of uncountable human beings wandering lost through the labyrinth of themselves because they have nothing to which to give themselves. All imperatives, all rules have been left in a state of suspension. The situation might seem to be ideal, since every man's life has been left entirely free to go its own way, to do as it pleases, to devote itself to itself. The same is true for every nation. Europe has relaxed its pressure on the world. But the result is altogether contrary to what might have been expected. Given over to itself, every life has remained immured in itself, empty, with no mission to fulfill. And since it must be filled with something, it "invents" or frivolously feigns a life, devotes itself to fraudulent occupations which impose upon it nothing meaningful. Today it is one thing, tomorrow another, the second the direct opposite of the first. It finds itself lost when it finds itself alone with itself. Egoism is labyrinthine; that is understandable. To live is to be impelled towards something, or at very least to progress toward a goal. The goal is not my progress, it is not just my life by itself; it is something I set for my life, so that it is something outside me, beyond me, further on. If I resolve simply to walk about within my own existence, egotistically, I make no progress, I go nowhere; I go round and about in the same spot. This is the labyrinth, a road that leads nowhere, which loses itself in itself because it is no more than an internal wandering.

After one war, the European shut himself up within himself and was left without projects for himself or for others. Thus we continue historically with no advance.

Sovereignty is not exercised in a void. It consists in a pressure exercised upon others. But that is not all, for then it would merely be violence. To command has a double purpose: someone is commanded, and he is commanded to do something. And what he is ordered to do is, in the end, to take part in an enterprise, in some great historic destiny. Hence, there is no imperium without a program for life, without a program for imperial life. As Schiller's verse says, "When kings build, carters have work."

It would not be right, then, to accept the trivial notion that pure egoism moves great nations, or men. It is not as easy as it seems to be a pure egoist, and no such person has ever reached the heights. The apparent egoism of great nations and men is merely the inevitable firmness natural to anyone who has his life set on a mission. When one has truly determined to carry out a large enterprise, it is hardly to be expected that much attention can be paid to chance altruism, to everyone who passes by. Travelers in Spain are oftentimes delighted by the reaction of people in the street to inquiries as to the whereabouts of a certain building or plaza. The person asked will often go out of his way and kindly offer to lead the traveler to the very place the stranger wanted to find. There is no doubt that the attitude displayed by the good Celtiberian contains a grand dash of generosity, and it is fortunate that the foreigner so interprets it. But every time I hear of such incidents I cannot refrain from a suspicion: Was the good Spaniard actually going any place at all? For the truth is that it might well often be that the Spaniard in those encounters is really going nowhere, has no purpose or project in mind, but has rather launched himself out into life to see if the lives of others will somehow fill his own with a bit of meaning. It even seems to me that my compatriots sometimes go out onto the street to see if they can perhaps find some foreigner to accompany to a desired destination.

It is a serious matter that doubt about hegemony and the whereabouts of authority in the world, hitherto held by Europe, should demoralize other nations — except for those who by reason of their youth are still in their prehistory. Even more serious is the completely demoralizing effect of this quietus, this marking time, upon the European himself. The fact that I am a European myself does not influence my position. I do not say that if the European no longer has a decisive role in the near future, the life of the world is no longer of interest. The end of European leadership and authority would not matter if there were some other group of nations ready and capable of taking its place. I would not ask that the new group assume power and the direction of the planet. I would be content if no one ruled, if such a situation did not entail the evanescence, the volatilization of all the virtues and qualities of European man.

And that is what would inevitably happen. If the European becomes habituated to forgoing his dominance, then the continent and after it the entire world would fall into moral inertia within a generation or two, into intellectual sterility and into universal barbarism. Only the hopeful anticipation of imperium and the discipline it entails could maintain and keep Western minds in the required state of tension. Science, art, and technology all live from and in the tonic atmosphere created by the consciousness and conscience of authority. If this be lacking, the European will become increasingly decadent and degraded. Western minds will no longer possess the profound and well-rooted faith in themselves which drives them to the pursuit of grand and new ideas in every order of life with characteristic audacity, energy, and tenacity. The European will become a creature of the day, quotidian. Incapable of creative, elaborate effort, he will fall back on yesterdays, on habit, on routine. He will turn into a commonplace, formula-ridden, empty creature, like the Greeks of the decadent age and those of the Byzantine epoch as a whole.

The creative life presupposes high discipline and fitness; it also requires constant stimulus to keep up the full consciousness of dignity. The creative life is one full of energy, and this is only possible when two conditions are met. Either the creator is in command or he is active in a world in which the person in command is one to whom he grants full right to command. One either commands or obeys. But to obey does not mean to put up with: to put up with is to be degraded. On the contrary, to obey requires respect for the one in command, and means following him with solidarity, with fervor to be serving under that command.

V

Let us return once again to the point of departure for this argument. And that is the curious fact that there is so much talk in these years about the decadence of Europe and the West. Now, it is another curious fact that this decadence was not first noticed by outsiders, but by Europeans themselves. It was their own discovery. When no one outside the Continent gave it a thought, it occurred to men in Germany, England, and France to wonder: Are we not beginning to decline?

The notion got a good press. And today everyone speaks of the decadence of Europe as if it were an incontrovertible fact.

But just interrupt the person proclaiming this doctrine and ask him on what concrete phenomena he bases his diagnosis. He is likely to make vague gestures encompassing the universe with his arms, as if he were the victim of a shipwreck. There is no spar to which he can cling. The only concrete data will probably be the series of economic difficulties besetting each nation, and even these may be relative. When the data are analyzed it will be found that none of it affects the power to create wealth; it will also be noted that the continent of Europe has passed through graver crises of this type in the past.

Do the Germans or English perhaps feel they are incapable of producing more and better than in the past? Not at all. It is important to be accurate about the state of mind of the Englishman or the German in this economic area. For the fact is that their undoubtedly depressed state arises not from their feeling themselves without capacity, but that, on the contrary, they sense they have more potential than ever and find themselves frustrated by false barriers which prevent them from carrying out what they could very well accomplish. The fatal frontiers of the economies of France, England, and Germany are caused by the political frontiers of these nations. The real difficulty, then, does not lie in the particular economic problems which arise, but in the fact that the form of public life in which economic potential must develop is inadequate to the magnitude of the possibilities. The feeling of diminution, of deterioration, of impotence, which undeniably oppresses and overcomes European vitality in these years comes from that disproportion between the magnitude of European potential and the framework of the political organization within which it must operate. The impetus to resolve the urgent and profound questions is as vigorous as it ever was, but it is obstructed by the small nations which form Europe, those little cages in which everything is housed.

The pessimism, the depression which invades the Continental soul is akin to that of a wide-winged bird which in beating its wings wounds itself against the bars of its cage.

The same condition is repeated on all levels, even though the factors are different from those on the economic plane. Take, for example, intellectual life. Every worthwhile intellectual in England, France, and Germany feels suffocated by the limits of his nation, feels his nationality to be an absolute limitation. A German professor senses the absurdity of the activity to which he is confined by his immediate circle of fellow professors and longs for the higher freedom of expression enjoyed by the French writer or the English essayist. Vice versa, the Parisian man of letters has come to realize that the tradition of literary mandarinism, of verbal formalism, to which his French birth condemned him, has been brought to an end. Now he would like to preserve the best qualities of his tradition, but would prefer to integrate it with some of the virtues preserved by the German professor.

In the internal politics of nations the same situation prevails. A definitive analysis has not yet been made of the strange phenomenon of the agony of political life in the great nations. Democratic institutions are said to have fallen into disgrace. But that is precisely what needs explaining, for it is a most curious fall from grace. On all sides, parliamentary institutions are denigrated. But no substitutes are put forth. Not even utopian forms of the state, which at least ideally might seem more desirable, are proffered. So: this apparent loss of prestige is not so authentic as it seems. It is not the institutions, the instruments of public life, which are malfunctioning in Europe; the trouble is with the ends to which they are put, or not put. There is simply a lack of purposeful programs consonant with the practical effective capacities that life has come to acquire for every European individual.

We have here an error in optics, indeed an optical illusion, which we should correct once and for all. It is painful to listen to the constant flow of absurdities about, say, the nature of parliaments. There are all kinds of valid objections to the way in which traditional parliaments conduct themselves; but if they are taken one by one, it will be seen that none of them justifies the conclusion that parliaments should be suppressed; on the contrary, they all suggest the need for direct reform. Surely, the best that can humanly be said of any institution is that it should be reformed, for that implies it is indispensable and that it is capable of new life. The automobile today is the result of all the objections made since 1910. But the popular cry against parliamentary bodies does not arise from such objections. It is said, for example, that such bodies are not efficient. Not efficient for what, we must ask? Efficiency is the quality an institution possesses to achieve its end. In this case, the end, the finality, would be the solution of the public problems of each nation. And thus we must insist that everyone who denounces the inefficiency of parliaments should have a clear idea himself of the needed solution to the public problems of the day. For if there is not, in a single country, a clear answer on what is to be done, even theoretically, then there is no point in accusing these institutions of being inefficient. It would be better to remember that never in history have any institutions created more formidable, more efficient states than did the parliamentary bodies of the nineteenth century. The fact is so indisputable that to ignore or forget it would be pure folly. Let us not confuse the possibility and urgent need for reform of legislative assemblies—so that they may become "even more" efficient and efficacious—with the denunciation of their "uselessness."

In short, the loss of prestige of legislative assemblies has nothing to do with their notorious defects. It proceeds from another cause, totally alien to the role of the assemblies as implements of public life. It is simply that they have not been put to proper use, and the end purposes of traditional public life are not respected; in short, the European has no illusion about the national states to which he belongs, and in which he feels a prisoner. If this much touted denigration of parliaments is examined closely, we shall see that the citizen in most countries has no respect for his state. It would be quite useless to alter details in the institutions, for these are not under fire; it is the state itself which has fallen short of expectations.

For the first time, the European, stymied in his plans—whether economic, political, or intellectual—by the limitations of his nation, feels that his vital possibilities, his lifestyle, are incommensurable with the collective body in which he is enclosed. He has discovered that to be English, French, or German is to be provincial. He finds himself, then, to be "less" than before, because previously the Englishman, the Frenchman, or the German thought himself to be, each one, a universe. Here we have the true source of the feeling of decadence which afflicts the European today. It is therefore a purely inner feeling and a paradoxical one, inasmuch as the presumption of decadence springs from the fact that his potential has increased while he is confined within an outmoded organization wherein he no longer fits.

As an illustration of this view, let us take a concrete example in the manufacture of automobiles. The automobile was a European invention, and nevertheless American production is superior. Thus we might say: the European automobile industry is decadent and in decline. Yet the European manufacturer—the industrialist and technician—realizes full well that the superiority of the American product is not due to some specific genius across the ocean but simply to the fact that the American factory can offer its product, without any restriction, to a market of some two hundred million buyers. Imagine a European factory being able to count on a market area composed of all the European states and their allies in the former colonies and protectorates. No one doubts that a car designed for five or six hundred million customers would be better and even cheaper than a Ford. All the good points of American technology are almost certainly effects and not causes of the scope and homogeneity of its ample market.

The "rationalization" of industry is an automatic consequence of the size of its market.

Europe's authentic dilemma, then, would appear to be the following: its long and splendid past has brought it to a new stage of existence where everything has been expanded and extended; but at the same time the structures handed down from the past seem dwarfed in the present and hinder new expansion. Europe has developed in the form of small nations. In a certain manner, the idea and sentiment of nationality has been its most characteristic invention. And now it finds it must exceed and surpass itself. Such is the outline of the enormous drama to be played out in the coming years. Will it be able to free itself of the structures made for the past or will it remain a prisoner within them forever? Once before in history a great civilization died out because it was incapable of building a substitute for its traditional idea of the state.

VI

I have recounted elsewhere the details of the death-agony of the Graeco-Roman world that are pertinent to our argument.* Now we can look at the death-throes from another aspect.

Greeks and Romans appear in history as lodged, like bees in their hives, within cities, the *polis*. We will take this to be an absolute fact, however mysterious in origin; we will take it as point of departure, without further ado, just as the zoologist starts from the bald, unexplained fact that while the sphex lives as a solitary wanderer the golden bee exists only in hive-building swarms.† Archeological excavation al-

---

* See the essay "Sobre la muerte de Roma" in *El Espectador*, VI, 1927.

† This is how physical and biological sciences reason, it is what constitutes "naturalist reason"; whereby they demonstrate that they are less reasonable than "historical reason." For the latter, when it

lows us a glimpse of what existed on the ground at Athens and Rome before the cities were there. But the transition from prehistory (purely rural and without specific character) to the springing up of the city (fruit of a new species which developed on both peninsulas), remains arcane. We are not even sure of the ethnic connection between those prehistoric peoples and the extraordinary communities which contributed a major innovation to the human repertory: that of constructing a public square and around it a city, shut off from the fields. The most accurate definition of the *urbs* and the *polis* much resembles the comical definition of a cannon: take a hole, wrap some metal stoutly around it, and there is your cannon. In the same way, the *urbs* and *polis* begin by being an empty space, that is, the *forum*, the *agora*. All the rest is a means of establishing the existence of the space, of assuring its outline. The *polis* is not primarily a complex of habitable houses but a place of civic assembly, a space set apart for public functions. The *urbs*, the city, is not built, like the cabin or the *domus*, as shelter from the weather and a place to procreate, which are private and family concerns, but is designed to discuss public matters. Observe that this development signified nothing less than the invention of a new kind of space, more novel than Einstein's space. Until then there was only one kind of space: the open country. People lived in the country, with all that such a way of life entailed. The man of the fields was still a sort of vegetable. His existence, all that he felt, thought, and wanted, preserved the unconscious torpor of a plant. The great civilizations of Asia were in this sense huge anthropomorphic vegetations. But the Graeco-Roman was determined to separate himself from

---

examines phenomena profoundly, and not merely obliquely as we do in these pages, refuses to recognize any fact as absolute. For "historical reason," *to reason* consists in making all facts fluid as well as in uncovering their genesis. See the author's essay *Historia como sistema* (R. de O., 2nd ed.).

the countryside, from "nature," from the geo-botanical cosmos. How was it possible? How can man withdraw from the country? Where will he go, since the country is the entire earth, one limitless field? Quite simple: he will mark off a portion of the field by means of walls, setting up an enclosed finite space over against limitless, amorphous space. Thus, the public square. It is not, like a house, an "interior" space enclosed from above as are the caves in the fields. It is purely and simply the negation of fields. The plaza or square, thanks to the walls enclosing it, is a portion of the countryside which turns its back on the rest: it places itself in opposition to the larger space. This smaller field secedes from the larger limitless fields and reserves itself to itself; it represents the annulment of the open country and is a space *sui generis*, a most novel kind of space, within which man frees himself from the community of animals and plants, leaving them outside and creating an ambience which is purely human. It is a civil space. Thus Socrates, the great townsman, quintessence of the spirit of the *polis*, can say: "I have nothing to do with the trees in the field. I have only to do with the men in the city." This spirit was unknown to the Hindu, the Persian, the Chinese, the Egyptian.

Up to the time of Alexander and of Caesar, respectively, the histories of Greece and Rome consisted of an incessant struggle between these two spaces: between the rational city and the vegetating countryside, between the lawgiver and the husbandman, between *jus* and *rus*.

Let it not be thought that this view of the city's origin is simply a personal idea or that it is merely symbolic. The inhabitants of the Graeco-Roman city retained, with extraordinary persistence, in the primary and deepest stratas of their memories, the recollection of a *synoikismós*. We need not consult the Greek texts, a translation will suffice. *Synoikismós* is an agreement to live together, consequently a joining or incorporation that is both physical and juridical. Vegetative dispersion over the countryside gives way to civil concentration in the city. The city is the super-house supplanting the infrahuman abode or nest; it is the creation of a more abstract and higher form of the familial *oikos*. It is the *res publica*, the *politeia*, made up, not of men and women, but of citizens. A new dimension, one not reducible to the primitive forms relating to the animal, is offered human existence, and those who were before merely men will now put their best energies into this novelty. The city, from the first instance already a state, comes into being.

In a certain way, the entire Mediterranean littoral has always displayed a spontaneous tendency towards this type of state. North Africa (where Carthage meant "The City") repeated the same pattern, with some variation. Italy did not emerge from the city-state until the nineteenth century. And the Spanish Levant falls eagerly into cantonalism, which is an aftertaste of that millennial inspiration.*

The city-state, because of its relatively small size, allows us to see clearly and specifically the principle of the state. On the one hand, the word "state" indicates that historical forces have achieved a combined and fixed equilibrium. In this sense it means the opposite of historic movement: the state has become a stabilized coexistence, constituted statically. But this quality of immobility, of defined form, conceals, as does all immobility or equilibrium, the dynamism which produces and sustains any state. It obscures the fact, so that one tends to forget it, that a state once constituted is merely the result of a previous movement, of the struggle and effort which went into its formation. The constituted state is preceded by the constituent state, and here we have a principle of movement.

---

* It would be interesting to trace the collaborative interplay of two antagonistic tendencies in the Catalonian region of Spain: one is European nationalism, the other the *urbanism* of Barcelona, in which the inclinations of ancient Mediterranean man persists. I have said that the man of the Spanish Levant is the remnant of *homo antiquus* in the Iberian Peninsula.

By this I mean to say that the state is not a form of society which man is given as a gift, but something he must laboriously build up. It is not like the organization of the tribe or other societies based on consanguinity which nature provides on her own without any human collaboration. On the contrary, the state commences when man strives to escape from the natural society within which he has been subjoined by blood. When we say blood, we could just as well say any other natural principle: language, for example. Originally, the state consists in a mixture of bloods and languages. It is the culmination of any and all natural society. It is hybrid and multilingual.

Thus the city is formed from the unions of diverse peoples. It establishes an abstract and homogeneous jurisprudence over a heterogeneous biology.* Still, this juridical unity is not the same as the aspiration which impels the creative movement leading to a state. That impulse is more substantive than mere legality; it constitutes a project involving vital enterprises greater than those possible to small societies related by blood. In the genesis of every state we can glimpse the figure of some great impresario.

If we observe the historical situation immediately preceding the birth of a state, we shall always find the following outline: various small communities with a social structure formed so that each might live inwardly within itself. The social forms serve solely for internal coexistence. And this indicates that each community had formerly lived in effective isolation, by and for itself without more than occasional contact with the neighbors on its limits. But this effective isolation was followed by a *de facto* external coexistence, especially on the economic level. The individual in each group no longer lived solely within the group: his life was now in part intertwined with individuals from other communities, and

* This juridical homogeneity does not necessarily imply centralism.

he dealt with them both in trade and in influence. There followed a certain disequilibrium between internal and external coexistence. The established social forms—laws, customs, religion—favor the internal structure and complicate the external development, which is newer and more ample. At this point, the principle of the state is a movement which tends to eliminate the social forms of internal existence, substituting for them a social form more adequate to the new and external coexistence. Applied to the present structure of Europe, these abstract expressions acquire a definite form and color.

The creation of a state is not possible unless the collective mind of certain communities has reached the point of abandoning the traditional structure of one form of coexistence and, more importantly, of imagining a form never before seen. And that is a matter of true creation. So: the state begins by being a work of absolute creativity. The imagination is the liberating power possessed by man. A people is capable of forming a state in the measure it is able to use its imagination. Hence, all peoples have shown a limit in their evolution of a state, precisely the limit set by nature to their imagination.

The Greek and the Roman, fully capable of imagining the city, which supercedes the dispersion of the countryside, could not go beyond the city walls. There were a few who wanted to extend the Graeco-Roman mind, to free it from the city alone, but the intent was unavailing. The clouded imagination of the Roman, represented by Brutus, took it upon itself to assassinate Caesar, the most creative mind of antiquity. It is very important for us to remember this episode, for we have reached the same chapter in our history.

VII

In speaking of men of great imagination, of what we can call men of vision, men capable of extraordinary clarity of thought, perhaps only two stand out in all the ancient world: Themistocles and Caesar, both of them men of polity, political men. And that is a truly surprising fact because the political man, even when famous, is political precisely *because* he is a bit coarse, and less than brilliant.* In Greece and Greater Rome there were thoughtful men of vision in many areas: philosophers, mathematicians, naturalists. But their clarity of thought was of a scientific order; that is, it was concerned with abstractions. Everything in which true science deals, whatever the science, is abstract, and abstractions are always clear and concise. So that the clarity of science lies not so much in the minds of scientists as in the matters with which they deal. Concrete vital reality, always unique, is the truly confusing and intricate element. And so, the authentically clear-headed man is the one who can orient himself in reality, the one who can perceive the hidden anatomy of the moment under the chaos present in every vital situation. In short, the man who does not get lost in the confusion of living is the one who is ultimately proven clear-headed. Consider those around you and see how they wander through life like sleepwalkers amid their good or evil fortune, without any suspicion of what is happening to them. And yet you will hear them speak in definitive formulas about themselves and their environment, and that would seem to indicate that they have some ideas about it all. But if these ideas are analyzed it will be seen that they scarcely reflect any of the reality to which they appear to refer. And if one goes deeper, it will be discovered that they are not even trying to adjust to reality. Quite the contrary: the person's "ideas" are merely the individual's blinders before reality, a way of avoiding the sight of his own life. For the truth is that life on the face of it is a chaos in which one finds oneself lost. The individual suspects as much, but is terrified to encounter this frightening reality face to face, and

* The meaning of this sudden affirmation, which presupposes a clear idea of what politics is, all politics—"good" as well as bad politics—can be found in the author's sociological treatise entitled *El Hombre y la Gente*.

so attempts to conceal it by drawing a curtain of fantasy over it, behind which he can make believe everything is clear. The fact that his "ideas" are not true does not worry him: he employs them as redoubts from behind which he can defend himself from life; or he uses them as a form of bravado to scare off reality.

The man with a clear view is the one who frees himself from phantasmagoric "ideas," and who looks squarely at life, realizing that all life is problematic. Inevitably, he feels himself lost. Since this is a literal truth — that to live is to feel oneself lost — whoever accepts the fact has already begun to find himself, to discover his authentic reality, and is already on firm ground. Like a shipwrecked castaway, he will look about for something to which he can cling; his tragically ruthless gaze and the profundity of his search for a means of saving his life will bring order out of chaos. For the only authentic ideas are those of the castaway. The rest is rhetoric, posturing, farce. Whoever does not really feel himself lost is lost without remission, that is to say, he never finds himself, never comes upon his own reality.

And this is true in all orders, even in science, though science be by nature an escape from life. (The majority of the men of true science devote themselves to it from fear of facing up their lives; they are not clear-headed men, hence their notorious ineptitude when confronted with concrete situations.) Our scientific ideas are of value in the measure that we have felt lost in the face of a question, have realized its problematic nature and have understood that we cannot get help from received notions, prescriptions, slogans, or mere words. The man who discovers a new scientific truth has first to pulverize almost all he has ever learned: he reaches the new truth with hands bloodied from the slaughter of innumerable commonplaces.

Politics is much more a reality than science, because it is made up of unique situations in which a man finds himself suddenly and perforce submerged. Thus it is an area where

we can best distinguish men of clear vision from those who
are prisoners of routine.

Caesar is the best example of someone with the capacity to
ascertain the essence of reality in a moment of fearful confusion, specifically at one of the most chaotic periods in the
history of humanity. It would seem that fate wished to emphasize this example of clarity, for simultaneously she brought
into being the mind of Cicero, a splendid exemplar of the intellectual, who spent his life making matters more confusing.

An excess of good fortune had dislocated the body of Roman political life. The city on the Tiber, mistress of Italy,
Spain, North Africa, of Classic and Hellenistic Greece, was
on the point of bursting. Its public institutions were bound
to the municipality, inseparable from the city, like hamadryads
attached to their tutelary trees, under sentence of dissolution
if they were to separate.

The health of democracies, whatever their type and degree, depends on a mere technical detail: the electoral process.
All the rest is secondary. If the conduct of elections is correct,
if it is in accord with reality, all goes well; if not, even though
everything else is in good order, all goes wrong. At the beginning of the first century B.C., Rome was all-powerful and
rich, without enemies in sight. And yet, Rome was at the
point of death because she insisted on maintaining a stupid
electoral system. (A stupid system is one which is unreal,
false.) Voting had to take place in the city. Citizens in the
countryside could not get to the elections, and even less could
those who lived scattered about the entire Roman world.
Since genuine elections were made impossible, it was necessary to falsify them, and the candidates organized gangs of
thugs—from among army veterans and circus athletes—whose
task was to disrupt the balloting.

Without the backing of an authentic suffrage, democratic
institutions remain in the air, where mere words dwell. Words
are things of air, and "the Republic was no more than a
word." The expression is Caesar's. No magistracy enjoyed

authority. The generals of the left and of the right—Marius and Sulla—were emboldened to set up empty dictatorships which led to nothing.

Caesar never elaborated his policy, but devoted himself, instead, exclusively to its execution. The policy was Caesar himself, not the manual of Caesarism, which was to come later. If we want to understand that policy we must simply apply his name to his actions. The secret lies in his major accomplishment: the conquest of the Gauls. To undertake this action he was forced to declare himself in rebellion against constituted power. There were reasons for this.

Power was in the hands of the partisans of the Republic, that is, the conservatives, who were faithful to the city-state. Their political stand may be summarized in two phrases. First, in their view the disturbances in the public life of Rome came about because of excessive expansion. The city could not govern so many nations. Every new conquest was a crime of *lèse-république*. Second, to prevent the breakdown of the institutions of the state a *princeps* was needed.

For us, the word "prince" has a meaning almost opposite to what *princeps* had to a Roman, for whom it meant a citizen like any other, but one invested with superior powers for the purpose of regulating the functions of republican institutions. Cicero in his *De Re Publica*, and Sallust in his memorial to Caesar, summed up the thought of all the political writers by requesting a *princeps civitatis*, a *rector rerum publicarum*, a *moderator*.

Caesar's solution was diametrically opposed to that of the conservatives. He realized that to remedy the consequences of previous Roman conquests, they had to be continued as before, and he fully accepted this stern destiny. Above all he urged conquering the new peoples of the West, who could be expected to be more of a threat in the not-too-distant future than the effete peoples of the East. In short, Caesar upheld the absolute necessity of bringing under Roman hegemony the barbarians of the West.

It has been said (by Spengler) that the Graeco-Romans were incapable of distinguishing the notion of time, of viewing their own existence as a projection or extension in temporality. They existed in the actual moment. I am inclined to think that this diagnosis is inaccurate, or at least that it represents a confusion of two entities. The Graeco-Roman did indeed seem surprisingly blind to the future. He did not see it before him, just as a color-blind person does not detect the color red. On the other hand he *was* rooted in the past. Before doing anything in his *now*, he took a step backward, like *Lagartijo*[3] as he went in for the kill in a bullfight. He sought a model for the present situation in his past and, duly satisfied with this knowledge, plunged into the waves of the troubled seas of the present, as if protected by a magical diving-bell. Hence in a certain manner he relived whatever he lived. He was archaic in style even in his present. And so were all men of antiquity. But that is not the same as being insensitive to time. It merely indicates an incomplete time-sense: an arrested development, an atrophy, of the sense of the future, an excessive development, a hypertrophy, of the sense of the past. The Europeans have always gravitated toward the future and feel it to be the most substantial dimension in time, which begins, for them, with "after" and not with "before." Thus, in the eyes of modern Western man, Graeco-Roman life seems timeless, outside time.

This near-mania for lifting the present, with pincers, out of a model past has been inherited from the man of antiquity by the modern philologist — or rather philologue[4] — who is also blind to the future. He, too, is retrograde and seeks a precedent for every present actuality; he calls this precedent, using his own particular idyllic language, his "source." I mention all this in connection with the fact that even the ancient biographers of Caesar blinded themselves to any understanding of this great figure by assuming that he meant to imitate Alexander. The equation was for them an inevitable one: if Alexander could not sleep from thinking of the laurels of Miltiades,

Caesar must perforce have suffered insomnia brooding on those of Alexander. And so backwards *ad infinitum*: always the step back, today's foot in yesterday's footprint. Our contemporary philological philologue recapitulates the classic biographer.

To imagine that Caesar aspired to repeat something that Alexander had already done—and such is the belief of most historians—is to renounce any attempt to understand him. Caesar is very nearly the opposite of Alexander. The only idea they shared was a vision of a universal imperium. But the idea is not Alexander's: it comes from Persia. The image of Alexander would have impelled Caesar toward the East and its prestigious past. His decided preference for the West demonstrates his determination to do something completely different from the Macedonian. Moreover Caesar had in mind more than a universal imperium: his deeper purpose was a Roman empire which did not depend on Rome but on the provincial periphery, and *that* implied moving beyond the city-state. It implied a state in which the most diverse peoples collaborate and with which all feel solidarity; it would not depend on a center to command nor on a periphery to obey, but would rather constitute an immense social body, in which each element would be at the same time both an active and a passive subject of the state. Such is the modern state, and such was the incisive vision of Caesar's futuristic genius. But it all presupposed an anti-aristocratic, extra-Roman power infinitely raised above the Republican oligarchy, above its *princeps*, who was solely a *primus inter pares*. This executive power, representative of a universal democracy, could only be a monarchy, with its center outside Rome.

Republic! Monarchy! These two words constantly change their *authentic* meaning at every stage in history, so that it . is necessary to reduce them to their elements at every stage and thus ascertain their ultimate sense.

Caesar's most trusted comrades, his confidential circle, were not archaic-minded city luminaries but new people, energetic and efficient provincials. His closest minister was Cornelius Balbus, an entrepreneur from Cádiz, a colonist and "Atlantic man."

But Caesar's vision of a new state was too advanced: the slow moving minds of Latium were not capable of taking such a leap. Their image of the city, with its tangible materialism, prevented the Romans from "seeing" the new organization of the body politic. They wondered how men who had not lived in a city could form a state. What was this new kind of unity, so subtle, almost mystical?

I repeat: the reality we call a state is not the spontaneous coexistence of men united by consanguinity. The state comes into being when naturally divided groups are obliged to live together. The unifying obligation is not one of brute force, but rather implies an initiating project, a common purpose offered to dispersed groups. Before all else, the state is a plan 'for action, a program for collaboration. Societies are called into being so that men may do something together. The state is not consanguinity, nor linguistic unity, nor territorial unity, nor is it contiguity of habitation either. It is not something material, inert, fixed, limited. It is pure dynamism — the will to do something in common — and thanks to this feature, the state has no physical limits.*

There was a sharp wit in the political emblem emblazoned by Saavedra Fajardo:[5] an arrow, and written beneath it "Either it rises or it falls." Such is the state. It is not a thing, but a movement. At every instant the state *comes from* and *goes to* somewhere. Like any movement it has a *terminus a quo* and a *terminus ad quem*. If a cross-section be taken at any given moment of any authentic state, a unity of coexistence will be seen which *appears* to be based on some material attribute: consanguinity, language, "natural frontiers." A static interpretation would lead us to say: "That is the State." But

* See the author's "El origen deportivo del Estado" in *El Espectador*, VII, 1930.

we soon observe that this human grouping is doing something or other in concert: overcoming another people or nation, establishing colonies of some sort, federating with other states; that is, at all times going beyond what seemed to be the material principle of its unity. This constitutes the *terminus ad quem* of the true state, whose unity consists precisely in superseding any given unity. When the forward impulse ceases, the state automatically succumbs and the unity which previously existed and appeared to be cohesive and binding—race, language, natural frontier—proves useless. The state comes apart, evanesces, breaks down.

Only this double aspect of the state's every moment—the unity which already exists and the more ample unity it proposes to establish—allows us to understand the essence of the national state. As we know, no one has yet explained what constitutes a nation in the modern sense. The city-state was a clear enough concept, obvious to the eyes in one's head. But the new type of public unity, which first appeared among the Germans and the Gauls, is a political invention of the West, and is much more fleeting and vague. The philologue, the historian of the moment, archaizing by nature, when confronted with this formidable development, finds himself almost as puzzled as Caesar and Tacitus when they tried to describe in Roman terminology the incipient states beyond the Alps or the Rhine, or even those in Spain. They call them *civitas, gens, natio*, fully aware that none of these names fits the measure.* They were not *civitas*, for the simple reason

* See Dopsch, *Fundamentos económicos y sociales de la civilización europea*, 2nd ed., 1924, II, pp. 3-4.
[Alfons Dopsch, *The Economic and Social Foundations of European Civilization*, condensed by Erna Patzelt from the second German edition and translated by M. G. Beard and Nadine Marshall (London, 1937), pp. 165-167. See also A. Dopsch, *Wirtschaftliche und Soziale Grundlagen der europäischen Kulturentwicklung* (2nd ed., Vienna, 1924; reprint Aalen, 1968), II, 1-4.]

that they were not cities.* And it was no use making the term a vague one and using it to designate a certain limited area. The new "nations" change terrain with the greatest of ease, or they enlarge, extend, or reduce it at will. Nor are they ethnic unities, *gentes, nationes.* However far back we go, the new states appear already formed by groups not connected by birth. They represent combinations of different bloodlines. What, then, is a nation, since it is not a community of bloodlines, or of attachment to territory, or anything of the sort?

As always happens, even as in this case, a sensitive acceptance of the facts provides us with the key. What is most obvious, what stands before our eyes, whenever we consider the evolution of any "modern nation" — France, Spain, Germany? Simply this: what at one period seemed to constitute nationality appears to be negated at a later date. At first, the nation seems to be the tribe, while the tribe next to it is still a nonnation. Later, the nation is made up of the two tribes, then it is seen as a region or territory, and a little later it is an entire county or duchy or "kingdom." León is a nation, but not Castile; then it is León *and* Castile, leaving out Aragon. Two principles are evident. The first, variable and continually superseded, is the tribe, the region, the duchy or kingdom, with its language or dialect; the second is more permanent and soars above linguistic and other limitations, proposing by way of unity that which was considered at the prior level to be in total opposition.

The philologues — my designation for those who nowadays style themselves "historians" — practice a bit of tomfoolery when they start from what the Western nations are today, from what they have become in our ephemeral era, at the end of the last two or three centuries, and suppose that Vercingetorix or El Cid Campeador[6] were already striving to build a

---

* No matter how densely clustered the dwellings, the Romans never referred to barbarian populations as cities. They called them, faute de mieux, *sedes aratorum.*

France stretching exactly from Saint-Malo to Strasburg or a
Spania reaching from Finisterre to Gibraltar. These philologues,
just like an ingenious Romantic playwright, describe their
heroes as setting off for a Thirty Years' War. In explaining
how France and Spain were formed, they assume that France
and Spain preexisted as entities in the French and Spanish
soul; as if they were French or Spanish from the beginning,
before the existence of France and Spain! As if the French or
Spanish were not the products of two thousand years of
travail!

The plain truth is that modern nations are simply the present manifestation of the above-mentioned *variable* principle, condemned in advance to continual displacement. That
principle of nationhood is not now based on "blood" or language, for the community of "blood" and language in France
or Spain is the effect and not the cause of the unification of
the state; this principle is now based on the "natural frontier."

It is all very well for a statesman to use this concept of
natural frontiers as a tool and weapon in the course of astute
negotiation, but a historian cannot entrench himself behind
that notion, as if it were a permanent redoubt. For it is neither permanent, nor is it even sufficiently definitive.

Let us not forget what the question is, strictly speaking. It
is a matter of ascertaining what the national state—what today we call a nation—really is, as distinct from other types of
state, like the city-state, or, at the other extreme, the Empire
founded by Augustus.* If the question is to be formulated
even more clearly and precisely, let us put it this way: What
is the force which has given rise to the coexistence of millions
of men under the sovereignty of the public power we call
France, or England, or Spain, or Italy, or Germany? It was

* We know that the Empire of Augustus is the very *opposite* of
what his adoptive father Caesar aspired to create. Augustus oper-
ated along the same lines as Pompey and the enemies of Caesar.
The best book to date on the subject is Eduard Meyer's *The Monarchy of Caesar and the Principate of Pompey* (1918).

not a prior community of race, for each of these collective bodies flows with torrents of blood from the most diverse sources. Nor was it linguistic unity, for the peoples now brought together in one state or nation spoke and still speak different languages. The relative homogeneity of language and shared physiognomy which they now enjoy—if it is a matter of enjoyment—are the results of previous political unification. Consequently, neither "blood" nor language creates the nation-state; rather it is the nation-state which levels the differences originating from the gene and the articulation of sound. And thus has it ever been. Rarely, if ever, has the state *coincided with a prior identity of "blood" or language.* Spain is not today a national state *because* Spanish is spoken throughout the country,* nor were Aragon and Catalonia nation-states *because* at a certain period, arbitrarily chosen, the territorial boundaries of sovereignty coincided with the boundaries of Aragonese or Catalan speech. We would be closer to the truth if, adapting ourselves to the casuistry which every reality offers us, we were to accept the following presumption: a linguistic unity embracing a territory of any extent was almost surely precipitated by some prior political unification.† The state has always been a grand impresario and dedicated matchmaker.

All this has been obvious for some time past, so that it is all the more extraordinary that "blood" and language should so persistently be designated as the foundation of nationality. There is as much ingratitude as inconsistency in these notions, for the Frenchman owes the existence of his present-day France, and the Spaniard his modern Spain, to an X

* It is not even true in actual fact that all Spaniards speak Spanish, any more than that all the English speak English or all Germans speak High German.

† Such phenomenon as *koine* and *lingua franca*, which serve as supra-national languages, are of course excluded from this consideration.

principal, the impulse for which was directed precisely toward surmounting the narrow community based on "blood" and language. Otherwise France and Spain would consist today of the very opposite of what made them possible.

A similar distortion is embodied in the attempt to base the idea of a nation on territorial shape, on the presumed discovery of a principle of unity not provided by "blood" and language, finding it instead in the geographical mysticism of "natural frontiers." Here again we confront an optical illusion, an error of vision. Today's chance boundaries mark off what we call nations stretching over wide areas of the continent or on adjacent islands. These boundaries are presumed to be "natural frontiers," and their "naturalness" is thought to signify a kind of magical predetermination of history by telluric form. But this myth evaporates when it is submitted to the same reasoning which invalidated the community of "blood" and language as the fount of nationhood. Here again, if we go back a few centuries, we find France and Spain separated into an array of lesser nations with the inevitable "natural frontiers." The mountain frontiers were less imposing than the Pyrenees or the Alps, the water barriers were less considerable than the Rhine, the English Channel, or the Straits of Gibraltar, but this only proves that the "naturalness" of frontiers is purely relative. It all depends on the economic and military capabilities of an epoch.

The historical reality behind this famous notion of a "natural frontier" consists in its being no more nor less than an obstacle to the expansion of people A over people B: for A it is an obstacle either to coexistence or to the ability to make war, while for B it is a defense. The idea of a "natural frontier," then, naively presupposes that the possibility of expansion and unlimited fusion between peoples is even more natural than any frontier. Only a material obstacle, apparently, prevents this natural development. The frontiers of yesteryear do not seem today to have been the basis of the French or Spanish nations, but rather the contrary: they were obstacles which the national idea had to overcome in the process of unification. And now, notwithstanding all experience, we still attempt to impart a definitive and fundamental character to today's frontiers, in spite of the fact that the new means of transport and of warfare have nullified their effectiveness as obstacles.

What part have frontiers played, then, in the formation of nationalities, inasmuch as they have not been the basic element? The answer is clear enough, and it is of the greatest importance for an understanding of the authentic idea of a nation-state as opposed to the city-state. Frontiers have simply served at every stage to consolidate the political unification already achieved. They have not been the *beginning* of a nation, but rather the contrary: at the *beginning* they were obstacles, and later, once overcome, they have been a definite means of buttressing unity.

In short, they have served the same purpose as language and notions of race. It has *not* been the indigenous community of one people or another which has *constituted* a nation, but rather the opposite: the nation-state, in its impulse and drive for unification, has always come up against the plurality of "races" and languages as against so many obstacles. Once these have been decisively overcome, a relative unification of "races" and languages has been effected by way of assuring and consolidating the general unity.

It is only right, then, to counter the traditional misconception attached to the idea of the nation-state and to accept the fact that the three ingredients which were thought to constitute nationality are actually the primary obstacles to it. (Undoing a misconception lays one open to the charge of being the victim of a misconception.)

We must resolve to search for the secret of the nation-state in its own specific and particular reason for being a nation-state, in its own inspiration and concept of polity, and not in extraneous principles, biological or geographical in character.

Why was it ever thought necessary to have recourse to race,

language, and territory in order to understand the phenomenon of modern nationalities? Purely and simply because in them we find a close and root-solidarity between individuals and the public power, one unknown to the classic state of old. In Athens and Rome the state consisted of a few individuals. The rest—provincials, colonials, allies, slaves—were mere subjects. No one, in England, France, or Spain, has ever been a mere subject of the state; each subject has been, rather, a participant in it, at one with it. The form, especially the juridical form, of this union with and in the state has been very different at different times. There have been great distinctions in rank and personal status, there have been classes relatively privileged and others relatively *un*privileged, but if the effective reality of the political situation in each period be interpreted and its spirit relived, it becomes evident that each individual felt himself to be an active subject of the state, both a participator and a collaborator. The "nation"—in the sense this word has evoked in the West for over a century now—signifies the "hypostatic union" of the public power with the collectivity it governs.

The state is always—whatever its form: primitive, ancient, medieval, modern—an invitation offered by one group of men to other groups for the purpose of carrying out some joint enterprise together. Whatever the intermediate aims, the enterprise in question will consist, in the long run, in organizing a certain type of life in common. The inseparable terms here are: the state and a project for coexistence, the state and a program of human activity or conduct. The different kinds of state come about in accordance with the different ways in which the promoting group enters into collaboration with the *others*. Thus, the ancient state never succeeds in fusing with the *others*. Rome rules and rears the inhabitants of the Italian peninsula and of the provinces but does not raise them to a union with itself. Even in the capital it does not bring about the political fusion of the citizens. It should not be forgotten that under the Republic, Rome was, strictly speaking, two Romes: *Senatus Populusque Romanus*, the Senate and the People. State communication never got beyond mere articulation between groups which remained outsiders and strangers to each other. Hence it was that the Empire, when threatened, could not count on the patriotism of the *others*, and had to defend itself exclusively by administrative and military measures of a merely bureaucratic nature.

The incapacity of the Greeks and Romans to bring about a fusion of their varied groupings arose from profound causes not to be examined here. Still, these causes may be summed up in one. Ancient classic man interpreted the collaboration which perforce characterized any state in a simplistic fashion: as a duality of governors and governed.* Rome's role was to command and not to obey; others were to obey and not to command. In this way the state was materialized with the *pomoerium*, within the urban body delimited by walls.

Later peoples brought with them a less material view of the state. If the state be a project for common action, its reality is purely dynamic: it is a *doing*, something to be done, the community in action. In this light, everyone forms an active part of the state and is a political subject, if he lends support to the enterprise — and race, blood, geographical location, social class are all matters apart and of secondary importance. What counts now is not past community, traditional and immemorial — in short, destined and unchangeable — but the community of the future with its effective action. Not what

---

* Confirmation of this attitude is to be seen in something which might at first glance be taken as a contradiction: the granting of citizenship to all inhabitants of the Empire. For it so happens that this concession was made at the very moment citizenship was losing the character of political statute and changing into service to the state and a burden, or a mere title in civil law. Nothing more might be expected from a state in which slavery was considered to be a matter of principle. In our "nations," on the contrary, slavery was only a residual fact.

we were yesterday, but what we are going to do together tomorrow, unites us together in the state. Hence the ease with which political unity in the West transcends the limits which enclosed the ancient state. For the European, in contrast to *homo antiquus*, behaves like a man facing the future, already living consciously in it, deciding his present conduct from the viewpoint of the future.

Such a political impulse will inexorably advance toward ever ampler unification, there being nothing, in principle, to impede it. The capacity for fusion is unlimited, not only that of one people with another, but what is still more characteristic of the nation-state, the unification of all social classes within each political body. As the nation grows, territorially and ethnically, internal collaboration increases. The nation-state is by nature democratic, and is so in a sense much more decisive than all the differences in the forms of government.

It is curious to note that when defining the nation by basing it on past community, Renan's formula is always accepted as best, namely, that the nation is "a daily plebiscite," for it adds a new dimension and attribute to those of blood, language, and common traditions. But is the meaning of this expression altogether clear? May we not provide a connotation quite different from the one suggested by Renan, an opposite meaning, which is, however, far truer?

VIII

In context, the well-known definition of a nation by Renan reads: "A nation is a great solidarity, constituted by the sentiment of the sacrifices that its citizens have made, and of those that they feel prepared to make once more. It implies a past; but it is summed up in the present by a tangible fact — consent, the clearly expressed desire to live a common life. A nation's existence is — if you will pardon the metaphor — a daily plebiscite. . . ."[7]

Such runs Renan's well-known judgment. How are we to

explain its widespread fame? Doubtless because of the graceful turn of the final phrase. The idea that the nation consists
in "a daily plebiscite" has a liberating effect on all of us.
Blood, language, and common past are static concepts; they
are inert, rigid, fatalistic; they imprison the imagination. If a
nation consisted in these elements and nothing more, the nation would be situated somewhere behind us, something we
need do nothing about. The nation would be something one
is or was, and not something one does or must do, and there
would be little reason to defend it even when attacked.

Whether we like it or not, human life consists of a constant
preoccupation with the future. At any present moment we
are concerned with the moment to come. So that living is
always, without pause or respite, a *doing*: something to be
done. Is it not obvious that *doing* means to carry out the
future, to real-ize it, make it real? This is true even when we
give ourselves up to remembering. We summon memory at
one moment to effect something in the next moment, even
if it be only the pleasure of reliving the past. This modest and
solitary pleasure, seemed, a moment ago, a desirable future
moment, and thus we *do* it, we *make* it. Nothing has any
sense for man unless it is related to the future.*

* From this viewpoint, humans are incurably futuristic in out-
look; that is, they live in the future and for the future. Yet, I have
contrasted ancient man with European man by saying that ancient
man is relatively blind to the future while modern Western man is
relatively far-seeing. Here we have an apparent contradiction. But
man is two-faceted: he is what he is, and he also has notions of
himself which may or may not coincide with his authentic reality.
Our ideas, preferences and desires cannot annul our true being, but
they can complicate and modify it. Both ancient classic man and
European man show the same concern with the future, but the
former subordinated the future to the dictates of the past, whereas
modern man gives greater leeway to the future, even to the new,
simply because it is new. This difference, not in essential being, but
as a matter of preference, justifies our calling European man a

If a nation consisted only in a past and a present, no one would be concerned with defending it against attack. Those who maintain the contrary are either hypocrites or simpletons. The truth is that the past of a nation projects its attractions — real or imaginary — into the future. A desirable future is one in which our own nation continues to exist. For that purpose we mobilize in its defense, not on account of language, or blood, or a common past. In defending the nation we defend our tomorrows, not our yesterdays.

This truth is what reverberates through Renan's phrase: the nation as a splendid program for the morrow. A plebiscite decides a future. The fact that in this case the future consists in the continuation of the past does not alter the matter in the least. It merely indicates that Renan's phrase is also archaic in nature.

Thus, the nation-state must represent a concept nearer to the pure idea of a state than to the ancient *polis* or the Arab "tribe" defined by blood. In point of fact, the national idea conserves no small commitment to the past, to the race, to the territory. And thus it is all the more surprising that the principle of unification of all citizens around a vitally attractive program always emerges as paramount. The ballast of the past, and that relative limitation within material principles, have never been and are not now completely spontaneous in the Western mind. They are rather the result of a learned interpretation of the idea of nationhood as conceived in the romantic tradition. If the nineteenth century concept of nationality had been current in the Middle Ages, nations such as

---

futurist, and classic man an archaizer. It is most significant that European man is no sooner aware of himself, no sooner becomes conscious of his role and assumes it, than he begins to speak of his time as the *"modern* epoch." 'Modern' means whatever is new and supersedes ancient usage. By the end of the fourteenth century, *modernity* is emphasized, especially in those matters which most concerned the period. For example, they spoke of *devotio moderna,* a kind of *avant-garde* in "mystical theology."

England, France, Germany, and Spain would never have been born.* For that interpretation confuses what constitutes a nation with what consolidates it. Let it be stated once and for all: it was not patriotism that created the nations. To believe otherwise is naive. Renan's definition presupposes as much. If, in order for a nation to exist, it is necessary that a community of men be able to count on a common past, what shall we call that same community when and while it lived in a present which from today's viewpoint is past? Evidently it was necessary that the common existence in question should die out, so that the community might then be able to declare "We are a nation." Do we not see here the embryonic vice of all the tribe of philologues and archivists, with their professional optical distortion, which prevents them from recognizing the sight of reality until it is past? The philologue is one who, to be what he is, requires the existence of a past before all else. A nation is another matter. Before it could count on a common past, it had to create its community and before creating it, had to dream it, will it, project it. And for a nation to exist, it suffices for it to have a future purpose, a project, even if it never be achieved, even if it be aborted, as has happened so often. We could give an example of the latter by speaking of Burgundy, for instance.

Spain shares a common past with the countries of Central and South America, a common racial background, a common language, and yet, it does not constitute a nation with them. Why not? There is one element lacking, the essential one: a common future. Spain was unable to develop a program for a collective future which might have attracted and involved nations so closely related. Moreover, the plebiscite for the future went against Spain. And so, all the archives, the common memories, the forefathers, the fatherland, served for nought. Where all these exist, they tend to encourage con-

---

* The principle of nationality is, chronologically, one of the first symptoms of Romanticism (at the end of the eighteenth century).

solidation,* and nothing more.

The nation-state, then, possesses a historical structure with a built-in plebiscite attached to it. All the rest appears to be transitory and changeable, and represents the form required by the plebiscite. Renan found the magic word, and it fairly bursts with light. It allows us to examine a nation's vitals cathodically, as it were, and we find that it is composed of two essentials. First, a project for total community based on a common enterprise. Second, the support of people for a compelling enterprise. This support, general in nature, produces the internal solidity which differentiates the nation-state from all the states of antiquity. In the latter, unity was produced and maintained by external pressure from the state upon disparate groups. In the new state, vitality is supplied by the all-encompassing cohesiveness of its "subjects." In reality, the subjects are now the state, and they scarce feel its presence: and that is the marvellous new quality of nationality.

And yet Renan very nearly nullifies the genius of his observation by applying it to a nation already formed, so that it must refer to its continuation. I would like to amend the phrase to make it apply to a nation *in statu nascendi*. That would make it a clearer insight. For in truth a nation is never wholly formed. In this it differs from other types of state. A nation is always in the process of making or unmaking itself. *Tertium non datur.* A nation is either gaining support or losing it, depending on whether the state is at a given moment projecting a vital enterprise.

Hence, it would be most instructive to recall the series of unifying enterprises which have successively buoyed Western humanity in the past. It will be seen how these endeavors have enlivened Europeans, not only in their public life, but

---

* We are now witnessing, as in a laboratory, a gigantic experiment. We shall see whether England is able to maintain an effectively sovereign unity of coexistence among the different parts of its former Empire, by proposing a compelling program for the future.

in their most private existence: they have either kept themselves "in training" for high purpose, or they have languished
and become demoralized and flabby, depending on whether
or not there were some vital undertaking in sight.

Such an examination would demonstrate another point as
well. State-enterprises of old, precisely because they did not
count on the close participation and support of the groups
among whom they were undertaken, and because the state as
such was always limited by a fatal narrowness—that of tribe
or a city—were paradoxically unbounded. A people such as
the Persian, Macedonian, or Roman might reduce to their
sovereign "unity" any portion of the planet they might con-
quer. Since such union was neither authentic, nor internal,
nor definitive, it was subject only to the military and administrative efficiency of the conqueror. In the West, however,
national unification has perforce followed a series of inexorable stages. We might well be more surprised that within Europe it has not been possible to establish an empire of a size
to match those of the Persians, of Alexander, or of Augustus.

The creative process for nations in Europe has always followed a certain rhythmic pattern. To wit:

First Phase: The particular Western instinct that makes of
the state a fusion of a variety of people into a unity of political or moral coexistence, is first felt in its actions and effects
upon those who are closest geographically, ethnically, and
linguistically. And that is not to say that this proximity is the
basis of the nation, but rather that diversity among neighbors
is the easiest to overcome.

Second Phase: In a period of consolidation, the *other* peoples beyond the limits of the new state are regarded as foreigners and more or less enemies. The national process takes
on an exclusivist aspect: the state turns inward, closes itself
off. In short, what we now call *nationalism* develops. In fact,
however, while the *others* are regarded as *politically* outsiders
and opponents, relations are established on an economic, intellectual, and moral plane. National wars serve to level tech-

nical and spiritual differences. Habitual enemies tend to become historically homogeneous.* Little by little there develops a consciousness that those enemy peoples belong to the same human circle as our own state. Still, they continue to be looked upon as hostile strangers.

Third Phase: The state enjoys full consolidation. At this point a new enterprise takes shape: to unite with those who until yesterday were its enemies. The conviction grows that we and they have moral affinities and common interests, and that together we can form a national front, a circle of defense against peoples even more foreign and more distant. The national idea has reached maturity.

One example will add clarification. It is often affirmed that in the time of El Cid Campeador, in the eleventh century, the idea of Spain (*Spania*) was already a national concept. The thesis is further fertilized by the recollection that centuries before the Cid, Saint Isidore had spoken of "Mother Spain." To my mind, all of this is a gross error in historical perspective. At the time of the Cid, the state of León-Castile was in the process of being formed, and this unity of the two kingdoms constituted the national idea of the time, the one politically effective idea. As for the concept of *Spania,* it was an erudite notion at best, one of those fruitful ideas sown in the West by the Roman Empire. The "Spanish" had grown accustomed to being linked together in administrative union by the Romans, as a *diocesis* of the Late Empire. But this geographic-administrative concept was a matter of accepting something from outside, not an inspiration from within, and in no way represented an authentic aspiration of the times.

However much credence one may want to give this eleventh century idea, it must be acknowledged that it never matched the definite and vigorous idea of Hellas attained by the Greeks of the fourth century. And then, even Hellas was not a true

---

* This homogeneity, however, generally respects and does not annul the plurality of original differences.

national aspiration. An authentic historical correspondence would more likely be the following: the idea of Hellas among the Greeks of the fourth century and of *Spania* among the "Spanish" of the eleventh and even the fourteenth century was analogous to the idea of Europe among the "Europeans" of the nineteenth century.

It is clear that attempts at national unity find their own right time, like sounds in a melody. Yesteryear's tendencies must wait for the morrow to take shape and form in the heat of an eruption of national aspirations. And their time is almost certain to come.

The time has now come for the *Europeans*: the time when Europe can be converted into a national idea. It is far less utopian to believe in this idea today than it was in the eleventh century to predict the unity of France or Spain. The more faithful the national state of the West remains to its authentic substance, the more truly will it perfect itself and emerge as a great continental state.

IX

The outlines of the original Western nations had scarcely been established when, within and around them, Europe itself emerged as their background. It is the common landscape in which they will move from the Renaissance on. And this setting, this European landscape, is formed by the nations themselves. Without noticing it, the nations will begin to eschew their bellicose plurality. France, England, Spain, Italy, and Germany will fight among themselves, form opposing alliances, dissolve them, and then form them again and regroup. But all of their activity, in war as in peace, represents a mutual coexistence as equals, something which Rome could never accomplish, either in peace or in war, with Gauls, Britons, Celtiberians, or the Germanic tribes. History has highlighted the conflicts, the politics in general, scarcely the most fertile soil for the seeds of unity. But while the fighting raged in one area, trading with the enemy proceeded in a hundred other areas; ideas were exchanged as well as art forms and articles of faith. In a certain sense the clash of arms was like a painted curtain behind which peace pertinaciously wove together the many-faceted lives of hostile nations. With each new generation spiritual homogeneity became more evident. To speak with greater exactitude and caution, we can put it another way: the souls and spirit of the French and the English and the Spanish may be and will continue to be as different as you like, but they possess a similar psychological structure; even more, they are building up a common content. More and more shared is the common stock of science, art, law, religion, social values, and even erotic lore. And these are the things by which men live. And a greater homogeneity is emerging than if all these peoples were cast in an identical mold.

An inventory now of the Western man's mental stock — opinions, standards, desires, assumptions — would reveal that most of it comes from a common European heritage, not from France alone for a Frenchman, not from Spain alone for a Spaniard, and so on. That which is European is more important than what is French, Spanish, or whatever. If the European were to imagine what it would be like to live alone with that which is merely "national" in him, and if he were to extirpate in fantasy all the foreign influences in his thinking and feeling, he would be horror-striken at the resulting emptiness. It would be clear that he could not possibly live on his own, for four-fifths of his spiritual endowment is the common property of Europe.

It is impossible to imagine any more important task for the European today than to fulfill the promise inherent in the concept of "European" during the past four centuries. The only obstacle to this destiny is the prejudice of the old "nations," the idea of nation as based on the *past*. We shall see, soon enough, whether the Europeans act like children of Lot's wife and persist in making history with their heads turned backwards. Our allusions to Rome, and to the men of the classic past in general, may serve as warnings: it is very difficult for a certain type of man to abandon the inherited notion of the state, once it has entered his head. Fortunately, the idea of the nation-state, which the European, consciously or not, brought into the world, is not the pedantic notion the philologue has preached to him.

A summation of the thesis of our essay is now in order. The world today is in the throes of a profound demoralization. One of its principal symptoms is the unprecedented rebellion of the masses. The immediate cause is the demoralization of Europe. One of the reasons for this, among many, is the displacement of the power which Europe formerly exercised over itself and in the world. Europe is no longer sure of itself, of its power to lead, and the rest of the world is unsure of wanting to be led. Historic sovereignty is in shreds.

There is no longer a "plenitude of the times," for that concept presupposes a clear, fixed, unequivocal future, like that of the nineteenth century. Then men thought they knew what was going to happen tomorrow. But nowadays there are too many incognitos on the horizon: there is no way of knowing *who* will rule or how power will be distributed in the world. By *who* we mean what people or group of peoples, of what ethnic character, and thus, of what ideology, what system of values, standards, vital resources.

The center toward which humanity will gravitate in the near future is unknown. Hence, life in the world has become scandalously provisional. Everything, everything done today in public or in private—even in inner consciousness—is provisional. The only exception is in some areas of some sciences. It would be wise to place no trust in any program nowadays praised, promulgated, or proclaimed. All of it will disappear more quickly than it appeared. All of it: from the mania for physical sport (the mania will subside, not the sport itself) to political violence; from "newest art" to overdone sunbathing at idiotic fashionable resorts. None of it, none of these novelties, has any roots. It is all sheer innovation and invention, in the worst sense of the words, which means that it is a matter of whim and caprice. These things do not well up out of the fundamental substratum of life; they do not represent authentic creation, nor any genuine impulse or need. In short: they are all vitally false, inauthentic representations of life. There is an innate contradiction in life-style: "sincerity" is cultivated and falsification is practiced. There is truth in existence only when we feel that our acts are irrevocably necessary. No politician today feels that his policies are inevitable; indeed the more extreme his attitude, the more frivolous are his acts, the less consonant they are with destiny. No life can be said to have its own roots, to be autochthonous, except one that is made up of inevitable sequences. All the rest, anything which we may take up or leave alone, anything for which we may be able to find a substitute, is a falsification óf life.

We live in an interregnum, in the empty space between two orders of historical rule, between what was and what is to be. Everything is essentially provisional. Men do not know in truth what institutions to abide, and women do not know in truth what men to abide.

Europeans cannot live unless they are involved in some great unifying enterprise. In the absence of such an enterprise, they become dispirited, enervated, and their spirit expends itself. The evolution of this process occurs before our very eyes. Those entities which up to now have been calling themselves "nations" reached their apogee a century ago. Nothing more can be done with them except to transcend them, move to something higher. They are no more than the substance of the past, accumulating around the European of today and weighing him down. We now enjoy more vital liberty than ever before, and yet the air in every European country is unbreathable, for it is confined air. What was formerly a nation, open to all the winds of heaven, has turned into some inland province. In the supranational Europe that we imagine, plurality should not and ought not to disappear. Where the state in antiquity annulled differences between peoples, or left them to wither in inactivity, or at best conserved them in mummified form, the national idea, more essentially dynamic, requires the active participation of that plurality, a plurality which has always been a *sine qua non* in the life of the West.

Everyone acknowledges the urgent need for a new principle of life. But, as always happens in similar crises, some people attempt to save the situation by an artificial cultivation of the very principle which has fallen into disuse. Hence the "nationalist" outbursts which have plagued the West in recent years. And thus it has always been. The last flare-up is the brightest, the last sigh is the deepest. On the eve of their disappearance, the frontiers, both military and economic, loom larger than ever.

All these nationalisms are so many blind alleys. Imagine projecting any one of them into the future. They become intolerable. They lead nowhere. Nationalism is counter to every instinct and impulse that led toward the creation of nations. Nationalism is exclusivist, the national principle is inclusivist. In periods of consolidation, nationalism has a positive merit and serves as a high and mighty standard. But in Europe, consolidation is long over, and nationalism is nothing but a mania, a pretext to escape from the necessity of inventing some great new enterprise. Its primitive methods of action and the type of man it exalts reveal abundantly that it is the very opposite of an act of historical creation.

Only the determination to construct a great nation out of the varied people of the Continent would give new life to Europe. It would once again believe in itself and would recover a sense of objective and disciplined purpose.

But the situation is fraught with more perils than is generally realized. The years pass and the European grows more accustomed to living life on a lower scale of value: he grows used to exercising no authority over himself or others. All of his higher capabilities are in danger of evanescing.

The conservative classes continue to oppose, as they have throughout the process of forming the various nations, the unification of Europe. Their recalcitrance could bring them to the brink of catastrophe, for there is a new menace over and above the definitive demoralization and sapping of the Continent's historical energy. It is a concrete and imminent threat. When communism triumphed in Russia, many observers expected Europe to be inundated by the Red tide. For my part, I never subscribed to that view. Quite the contrary: in those years I wrote that Russian communism was a substance which Europeans could not assimilate, for they are of a breed that through its history has devoted all its energy and fervor to the cause of individualism.

Time has passed, and the fearful ones of yesteryear have been tranquilized — just at the very moment when they have every reason to lose all tranquility. Because now, precisely now, the overwhelming drive of communism might well flatten out all of Europe.

Now, as before, the communist creed *à la Russe* does not attract or even interest the European, nor does it hold any worthwhile promise for the future. And this is so not for the trivial reasons alleged by the Red apostles — who are, like all apostles, headstrong, deaf, and no lovers of truth. Even the European *bourgeois* knows that, even without the advent of communism, the *rentier*, the man who lives exclusively off his revenues and rents and who hands these on to his heirs, has his days numbered. It is not this fact which immunizes Europe against the Soviet faith, and still less is it a generalized fear. The arbitrary postulates of Sorel[8] in the early part of the century advocating his tactics of violence now strike us as quite ridiculous. The *bourgeois* is no coward, as Sorel thought he was, and at this juncture he is more disposed to violence than the working man. Everyone knows that bolshevism triumphed in Russia because there was no *bour-*

geoisie. * Fascism, a *petit bourgeois* movement, showed itself to be more disposed to violence than all the labor movements put together. None of the above would serve to keep the European from having a fling with communism; he does not do so for another reason. It is simply that the European does not see in communist organization any increase in human happiness. And yet, in the future, Europe might very well grow to like the idea of communism. Not for the dogma itself, but despite it.

Let us imagine that the herculean "Five-Year Plans" of the Soviet government not only restore the gargantuan economy of Russia, but that they even succeed in making it burgeon. Whatever its essence, Soviet bolshevism represents a gigantic human enterprise. In its undertaking, men have resolutely determined on a destiny involving reform, and they live with and under the tension which the high discipline of their faith provides them. If the force of nature, unyielding to man's enthusiasm, does not frustrate their purpose and abort their efforts, if it leaves them a bit of scope, the wondrous daring of their endeavor might well shine over the European continent like a new and radiant constellation. If Europe, meanwhile, continues to vegetate and persists in its ignoble posture, its nerves flaccid from want of self-discipline, and from the lack of any project for a new life, how can it withstand the contaminating influence of the dynamic Red undertaking? It would be vain to expect the European to hear the siren call of some new program of *action* and not to respond to it, when currently he has no high standard of his own to hold aloft. For the sake of serving something which would give meaning to his life and allow him to sidestep his own existential void, the modern European might well swallow his objections to communism, and find himself drawn along, not by

---

* This sole fact should suffice to convince us once and for all that Marx's socialism and bolshevism are two separate historical phenomena with scarcely a common denominator.

the substance of this faith, but by its moral stance.

I see the building of a great national European state as the one and only enterprise that could counterbalance the attractions of any and all "Five-Year Plans."

Experts in political economy hold that there is little probability of success for the Russian economic plans. But it would be altogether too inglorious for the non-communist side to wait passively for a Russian collapse, as a way of overcoming these adversaries. The failure of the Russians would represent a universal failure for one and all, of man as such. Communism is a piece of "moral" extravagance, but it is nonetheless a species of morality. Would it not be more worthy and fruitful to offer, in opposition to the Slavic morality, a new morality for the West, a new program for life on earth?

15

We Come To The Real Question

THIS IS THE question, and the real problem: Europe has been left without a moral code. It is not that the mass-man merely denigrates an antiquated code in favor of a newly emergent one, but that at the center of his scheme of life there is the desire to live without conforming to any moral code whatsoever. Do not believe a word of what you hear from youth when they talk about the "new morality." I flatly deny that there exists anywhere a single group truly inspired by any new *ethos* showing signs of being an authenic moral code. When people talk of the "new morality" they are only committing a new immorality and looking for the easiest way of introducing contraband goods.

Hence it would be ingenuous simply to condemn the man of today for his lack of morality. The accusation would leave him cold, or rather it would tickle his fancy. The creed of immorality has become commonplace and anybody and everybody may boast of practicing the new rite.

If we leave out of the argument, as we have throughout, all those groups which represent survivals from the past — Christians, "Idealists," the classic liberals — there cannot be found anywhere among all the representative sectors of the present period a single group whose attitude to life goes beyond claiming all the rights and none of the obligations. It matters not whether the group is labeled revolutionary or reactionary: actively or passively, after a certain number of twists and turns, its state of mind will be seen to consist, in its decisive part, in ignoring all obligations and in feeling itself to be, without the slightest noting even in its own mind of any why, the legitimate heir to unlimited rights.

Whatever the influence on such a soul, the end-result to-day seems to be the same: a reason and pretext is found for not submitting to any concrete moral purpose. If this attitude appears under a reactionary or antiliberal sign, it will affirm that the salvation of the Fatherland, of the State, gives it the right to level all other standards, to flatten one's neighbor, especially if one's neighbor happens to be an outstanding personality in his own right. But the same thing happens if the mass-soul decides to act the revolutionary: the apparent enthusiasm for the manual worker, for the afflicted, for social justice, serves as a mask to disguise the rejection of all obligations—such as courtesy, truth-telling, and, above all, respect for and just estimation of the superior individual. I know of people who have joined one or another left-wing party solely to gain for themselves the right to despise higher intelligence and to avoid the need to pay it any respect. As regards contemporary dictatorships, we have seen only too well how they flatter the mass-man by trampling on everything eminent and above the common level.

This evasion of all obligation explains in part the phenomenon, half ridiculous and half disgraceful, of the promulgation of the platform of "Youth," of youth per se. Perhaps our times offer no spectacle more grotesque. Almost comically, people call themselves "young," because they have been told that youth has more rights than obligations, since the fulfillment of obligations can be postponed until the Greek calends of maturity. Youth has always considered itself exempt from *doing* or already *having done* great deeds or feats. It has always lived on credit. This has always been understood as being in the nature of humanity, a kind of feigned right, half ironic and half affectionate, conceded to their juniors by the no-longer young. It is astounding to behold that nowadays these juniors take it as a definitive right precisely in order to lay claim to all the other rights which belong only to those who have already accomplished something.

Though it may appear incredible, "youth" has become a form of blackmail. We are in fact living at a time of universal blackmail, and it is manifested in two complementary ways. There is the blackmail of violence, and the blackmail of caricature. Both forms have the same purpose: to make it possible for the mass-man to feel himself exempt from all subordination.

It will not do, then, to dignify the present crisis by presenting it as a conflict between two moralities or civilizations, one in decline and the other in ascent. The mass-man is simply lacking in any morality. For morality is always and essentially a feeling of subordination and submission to something, a consciousness of obligation and service. But perhaps it was a mistake, above, to use the word "simply." For it is not merely that this new type of creature is able to do without morality. No, let us not make it so easy for him. Morality cannot be simply ignored. *Amorality*—a word which lacks even a proper construction—does not exist. If one wants to avoid submitting to any norm, one must, *nolens volens,* submit to the norm of denying all morality. And that is not amorality, but immorality. It constitutes a negative morality which conserves the empty form of the other morality. How has it been possible ever to believe in the "amorality" of life? Doubtless because all of modern civilization and culture lead to that conviction. Europe is now reaping the painful consequences of its spiritual conduct. For Europe has given itself over to a magnificent but rootless culture.

This essay has been an attempt to sketch a certain type of European, particularly by studying his behavior in the civilization into which he was born. The analysis was necessary because this modern individual is not representative of some other civilization contending against his own older one. He himself is a mere negation of that civilization, a negation concealing what amounts to parasitism. The mass-man is still living precisely from what he denies and rejects, and from what others constructed or accumulated. Thus it was not pertinent to invoke his psychological portrait when raising the main question, which is: What root-defects beset modern European culture? For it is evident that in the long run the new type of human being now dominant in the world was born out of these defects and insufficiencies.

This larger question must remain outside the present pages, for it is exhaustive. An answer would require a detailed discussion of the doctrine of existence, which, like counterpoint or a *leitmotiv,* is already interwoven, insinuated, and suggested in all the above pages. Perhaps before long it can be shouted aloud.

Editorial Notes

Introduction

1. In an academic *tour de force*, the American scholar Nelson Orringer has traced Ortega's German sources, phrase by phrase, in an opus written in Spanish: *Ortega y sus fuentes germánicas*, Madrid, 1979. Erudition here leads to denigration of rival scholars and, inevitably, along with the revelation of the many primal sources, to a comparative slighting of Ortega's originality.

2. As to Ortega and anthropology, we may note his precursorship in one important regard: before Husserl concluded that phenomenology, strictly speaking, must become anthropological (in a letter to Levy-Bruhl), Ortega had already introduced his method of "vital reason" into phenomenological ideation, and thus "submerged it in the waters of life" (cf. Manuel Granell, *Ortega y su filosofía*, Madrid, 1960, p. 16.)

1. The Crowd Phenomenon

1. *the public life of the West*: The original has "Europe," but the entire book's tenor makes clear that the West is what is under consideration, as is the case in *The Decline of the West*, by Oswald Spengler, to which Ortega refers more than once.

2. *Minerva*: The goddess of wisdom. Ortega is here stressing the fact that the world is *always* wondrous to a pair of wide-open eyes, by citing the Athenian's choice of the never-blinking owl as Minerva's emblem.

3. *the most radical division to be made of humanity is between two types*: For a variant division, known to Ortega, cf. Zarathustra's speech "On the Three Metamorphoses" in Nietzsche's *Thus Spoke Zarathustra*: the camel who asks "What is difficult?" and reverently

kneels to take on and carry the weight of the spiritual achievements of the past; the lion who rears up against the past and declares his freedom from it; and the child, the "self-propelled wheel" who creates new values for mankind.

4. *must cease being part of the mass*: Ortega's minority/mass distinction, like Nietzsche's master/slave distinction, a concept the former knew intimately, was operative for them both at every social level.

5. *the "public," that is, the mass*: A novel definition of the difference between *public* and *mass* is supplied by Marshall McLuhan, the electric-informational-media populist and environmentalist: "Print technology created the public. Electric technology created the mass." Marshall McLuhan with Quentin Fiore, *The Medium is the Massage* (New York, 1967), p. 68.

A sex is supplied to multitudes, masses, by Ortega's contemporary, Miguel de Unamuno: "Multitudes are feminine. Bring men together, and you can be sure that it is the feminine side of their character, what they have of their mothers, that joins them and holds them together." Miguel de Unamuno, *The Life of Don Quixote and Sancho*, in *Our Lord Don Quixote*, trans. by Anthony Kerrigan (Princeton, NJ, 1967 and 1976), p. 293. A note by the translator adds "Multitudes *are* feminine in the Romance languages: e.g., in Spanish, *las muchedumbres*." And *las masas*.

6. *Today, "everybody" means the mass, the masses — and only the masses*: Speaking of the last half of the last paragraph, Gabriel Marcel, the French existentialist, writes: "These words of Ortega's are, it seems to me, one of the most lucid diagnoses that have been made of the sickness of our contemporary world." *Man Against Mass Society*, trans. by G. S. Fraser (Chicago, 1952), p. 104.

2. The Rise of the Historic Level

1. *Spengler*: Oswald Spengler (1880-1936), the great German historian, according to whom cultures undergo a cyclic development in an organic pattern similar to that of man's birth, maturity, and final decline into death. His master work was *Der Untergang des Abendlandes* (Munich, 1922-23); *The Decline of the West*, trans. Charles Francis Atkinson (New York, 1929). Ortega, like most of the thinkers of his day, paid him much attention and re-

ferred to him throughout his writings, though he rejected the concept of the West's "decline." Every type of contemporary writer, from James Joyce to F. Scott Fitzgerald (who said he read Spengler "and never got over it") was influenced by his worldview.

2. *"The happy few"*: In English in Ortega's text. Cf. *Henry V*, 4, 3:

> We few, we happy few, we band of brothers;
> For he today that sheds his blood with me
> Shall be my brother.

3. *Memoirs of The Comtesse de Boigne:* Charlotte D'Osmond, Comtesse de Boigne (1781-1866), was the hostess of one of the more important salons in Paris during the early nineteenth century.

4. *He is to history what sea-level is to geography*: Cf. Oswald Spengler, who suggests that the "masses," especially the peasant masses of history, are like ever-present fields of wheat.

5. *The decadence of Europe indeed!*: For a discussion and comparison of the word, "decadence," and others of the same order in the same context: "Western civilization has been shrinking; and the number of persons relative to the world population that the West rules have much and rapidly declined. . . . To speak of the 'decline' of the West is dangerous. It calls to mind Spengler, via the English translation of his title; and almost unavoidably suggests a psychological or moral judgment that may be correct but is irrelevant. . . . It is not self-evident that in shrinking quantitatively the West is morally deteriorating. Logically, the contrary might equally be the case. There are similar confusions with words like 'ebb', 'breakup', 'waning', 'withering', 'decay', 'crumbling', 'collapse', and so on. It may be of some significance that nearly all words referring to quantitative decrease have a negative feel when applied to human beings or society. But let us try to be neutral. Let us say only: 'Western civilization has been contracting'; and speak of 'the contraction of the West.' " James Burham, *Suicide of the West* (New Rochelle, New York, 1964), p. 21.

3. The Level of the Times

1. *the level of the times*: Ortega here and throughout makes use of an expressive phrase, *la altura de los tiempos*, common enough in Spanish, but without an English equivalent in ordinary usage.

We have paraphrased freely, omitting the original's "a phrase full of good sense which is senselessly repeated," inasmuch as in English no one "senselessly repeats" this sensible phrase.

2. *Jorge Manrique*: Spanish poet and soldier (1440-1478). The quotation is from his best known poem, *Coplas por la muerta de su padre Don Rodrigo*, the famous elegy on the death of his father.

> *Cualquier tiempo pasado*
> *fue mejor*

We add "far," without apology, to round out the poetic line and give weight to the English phrase.

3. *Alcheringa*: literally: dream-time. Now used as an anthropological term. Among primitive Australians, it referred to the time of mythical tribal ancestors. It also suggests all supernatural power, the animate force in nature.

4. *Horace*: (65-68 B.C.) Roman poet and satirist. We cite *The Odes and Epodes* in a bilingual edition, with English translation in prose by C. E. Bennett, The Loeb Classical Library (London and New York, 1919), Book III, 6, p. 203.

> *damnosa quid non imminuit dies?*
> *aetas parentum, peior avis, tulit*
> *nos nequiores, mox daturos*
> *progeniem vitiosiorem.*

5. *Trajan in his famous letter to Pliny . . . it would not be "in keeping with the spirit of our times"*: The Latin original is: *Nec nostri saeculi est.* The word *saeculum* can be defined as "the spirit of the age, of the time" (*Cassell's New Latin Dict.*). The German *Zeitgeist*, "the spirit of the time," perfectly expresses the meaning here. We might also speak of the "tone of the times."

6. *a devotee of history*: Ortega is speaking primarily of himself.

7. *a power similar to cosmic energy . . . the energy which . . . drives . . . the stars to shine*: Ortega read Nietzsche; cf. the latter's doctrine of Will-to-Power.

4. The Increase of Life

1. *absurdity in the world*: the phrase recalls the absurd universe of Camus. Space and time are the conditions of existence, which is absurd, i.e., devoid of intelligible structure. By contrast, being (essence), at least according to Plato, is intelligible, eternal, and at rest.

2. *a certain unease which will put him on guard*: Some years later, Sartre was to speak of this unease as ' nausea" — the experience of existence. Recall that Roquentin, the hero of *Nausea*, flees from M. Fasquelle's café crying "Anything can happen, anything can happen."

5. A Statistical Fact

1. *Werner Sombart*: (1863-1941), German social historian and economist, professor at the University of Berlin. Much of his work was in response to Marx, dealing primarily with the role of social class in European history.

2. *Rathenau*: Walther Rathenau (1867-1922), German industrialist, social theorist, and statesman, foreign minister of the Weimar Republic at his death; he was assassinated by anti-Semitic fanatics, Rathenau being a Jew. In his book *The New Society*, he opposed mechanization of the world, and state socialism; he argued for decentralized democratic social order in which production and distribution would be administered by consumer-producer guilds.

7. Noble Life and Common Life, or Effort and Inertia

1. *The mass-man would never have looked to a higher authority than himself. . . . [He] feels himself lord of his own existence. The select man . . . is impelled to seek a norm higher and superior to himself*: The entire passage, indeed these pages as a whole, are redolent of the influence that Thomas Carlyle was having in Spain all through Ortega's early years. Miguel de Unamuno, the prime influence on Ortega before he went to Germany, began his career in literature with a translation of Carlyle's *The French Revolution*, and the book had an enormous impact in Spanish. It is more elucidating to compare even the first pages of Carlyle with Ortega at this point: "Neither was that an inconsiderable moment when wild armed men first raised their Strongest aloft [and] said solemnly: Be thou our Acknowledged Strongest! In such Acknowledged Strongest . . . what a Symbol shone now for them. . . . A Symbol of true Guidance in return for loving Obedience; properly, if he knew it, the prime want of man." And: "The nobles . . . have nearly ceased either to guide or misguide; and are now, as their master is, little more than ornamental figures. It is long since they have done with butchering one another or their king. . . . Close

viewed, their industry and function is that of dressing gracefully and eating sumptuously." Thomas Carlyle, *The French Revolution*, pp. 7, 10. A massive mix-up of mass-men!

2. *Nobility is to be defined by exigencies and obligations, not by rights*: The German sources of Ortega's view of nobility have been exhaustively documented. Nelson R. Orringer has pointed out the influence of Johannes Maria Verweyen (1883-1943), a philosophy professor at Bonn: from him "have come most of Ortega's formulations for his definition of nobility in *La rebelión de las masas*"; and, "in essays antedating his reading of Verweyen, Ortega has acknowledged a debt to Nietzsche for the idea of nobility as the dutiful effort to surmount oneself. But the remainder of Ortega's definition, as it appears with more completeness and precision in his book, virtually condenses the introduction to Verweyen's study *Der Edelmensch und seine Werte*, first published in 1919." Orringer adds that the second edition (1922) is to be found in Ortega's personal library, and this is the edition he apparently read. Nelson R. Orringer, "Nobles in *La rebelión de las masas* and Related Works: Ortega y Gasset's sources," *The American Hispanist* 1, No. 5 (Jan 1976), pp. 601–02.

8. Why the Masses Intervene in Everything and Why They Always Intervene Violently

1. *Syndicalism*: A social and political movement advocating that trade unions take over and exert direct control of the means of production. This movement frequently took the form of anarcho-syndicalism, which emphasized the use of nonelectoral, nonparliamentary means—such as the general strike—to achieve its goals. These recommended forms of activity were often referred to as "direct action." Anarcho-syndicalism was especially strong in Spain and other countries in Latin Europe in the late nineteenth and early twentieth centuries.

2. *the reason of unreason*: Although there are overtones of a long Spanish tradition of irrationalism whenever Ortega speaks of "unreason," he is often speaking concretely of the philosophical bias of his first great influence, Miguel de Unamuno, who preferred Spain to have had a Teresa of Avila in its past rather than a Descartes. In his *The Tragic Sense of Life*, published in 1913, Unamuno

had proclaimed that "reason is the enemy of life," for the living being is unstable, individual—and unintelligible. Unamuno "had given irrationalism its most forceful, intense, impassioned, effective, and perhaps happiest formulation" (in the words of Julián Marías in his *José Ortega y Gasset: Circumstance and Vocation,* trans. Frances López Morillas [Norman, Oklahoma, 1970], p. 465). Unamuno refined the concept of irrationalism to the point where he held that "everything which is vital is anti-rational, and not merely irrational, and everything which is rational is anti-vital." Ortega developed his theory of vital reason as an answer to this irrationalism, by which he was fascinated, and his theories were a direct outgrowth of the contrasting currents in Spanish thought. Both Unamuno and Ortega, it should be noted, were in agreement in standing against sterile *rationalism*.

10. Primitivism and History

1. *Kurt Breysig:* (1866-1940), Berlin professor who attempted to formulate developmental laws of universal history, according to which humanity ascends to ever higher cultural levels. See his *Kulturgeschichte der Neuzeit* (Berlin, 1900).

11. The Age of Self-Satisfaction

1. *The Catholic who gives . . . adherence to the Syllabus:* The *Syllabus of Errors* was attached to the encyclical *Quanta cura* issued by Pius IX at the end of 1864. It listed eighty of "the principal errors of our time." The eightieth was the most famous, and it stigmatized as error the notion that "the Roman Pontiff . . . should reconcile himself to and agree with progress, liberalism, and modern civilization." In context, the reference was to the then new Italian kingdom, and any compromise with it. Though it undermined the position of liberal Catholics, it did not hold that intolerance was universally valid, but rather that the concept of toleration as a final and universal answer was itself invalid.

13. The Greatest Danger: The State

1. *Fouché's contrivances:* The passage—incorporating the quotation from Ward—here is taken from Élie Halévy, *A History of the*

English People in 1815, trans. E. I. Watkin and D. A. Barker (New York, 1924), I, 39. A footnote cites *Letters to Ivy*, Dec. 27, 1811, [*Letters to 'Ivy' from the First Earl of Dudley*], by John William Ward, First Earl of Dudley (1781-1833), English M.P. and eccentric.
Fouché: Joseph, Duc D'Otrante (1759-1820), French statesman and organizer of police. He served every French government from 1792 to 1815, despite all the violent changes. First a seminarian, he became a Jacobin and an agent for "de-Christianization." Later, he organized the secret police under Napoleon. He was a royalist and minister of police under Louis XVIII, but was proscribed as a regicide in 1816.

14. Who Rules the World?

1. *Waldo Frank* (1889-1967), American novelist and social critic. *The Re-discovery of America* (New York, 1929) was first published serially in *The New Republic* in 1927-28.
2. *every half-baked brand-new nation*: The Trinidad-born Indian writer V. S. Naipul calls these nations "half-made": "half-made societies that seem doomed to remain half-made." He also speaks of some of the "Third World" nations as countries "without history." Speaking of the break in tradition he describes "the new politics, the curious reliance of men on institutions they were yet working to undermine." *The Return of Eva Perón; with the Killings in Trinidad* (New York, 1980), passim.
3. *Lagartijo*: Rafael Molina Sanchez (1841-1900), Spanish *torero*. Though there were several toreros who used this nom-de-guerre, Ortega doubtless had in mind this phenomenal figure who dispatched nearly five thousand bulls in disciplined and artistic encounters. He donned a torero's costume at age nine and was a master at twenty-four. He was one of the most elegant and complete toreros of all time. The torero Antonio Ordoñez has said of Lagartijo: "He is one of those artists who have reached closest to pure perfection, that entelechy which, if it were fully achieved, would bring us to absolute nothingness [*la nada absoluta*]." Antonio Abad et al, *Los Toros* (Barcelona, 1966), pp. 424, 430.
4. *the modern philologist — or rather philologue*: Ortega's word is "*filólogo*," whose exact translation is "philologist." But a little later in the text Ortega states that he uses the word to designate

contemporary "historians." Given this idiosyncratic meaning, we have translated it by a word as original as his peculiar definition.

5. *wit in the political emblem emblazoned by Saavedra Fajardo*: Saavedra Fajardo, Diego de (1584-1648), Spanish diplomatist and man of letters, best-known for his "anti-Machiavellian emblem book" (*Ency. Britt.*), *Idea de un príncipe cristiano* (1640), which urged a return to tradition to avoid decadence.

6. *El Cid Campeador*: Rodrigo Díaz de Bivar (c. 1043-1099), most renowned of medieval Spanish soldiers, known as "El Cid Campeador," Lord Battle-Winner. He is the subject of much epic literature, especially as the legendary hero of *El Cantar de Mio Cid*. He excercised his inspired generalship on several sides in the continual wars between Moors and Christians, and between Moors under diffferent Christian protectorates. He also made war on the Moors independently, as in his conquest of Toledo and, more importantly, though also ephermerally, in his conquest of the Moorish kingdom of Valencia.

7. *"A nation is . . . a daily plebiscite. . . . "* The translation given here from the French is from Ernest Renan, *The Poetry of the Celtic Races, and other Studies*, trans. William G. Hutchison (London, n.d.), p. 81.

Ernest Renan (1823-1892), French historian and philosopher, evolved a personal Christianity, based on social and historical movements and on his individual views on religious origins seen and examined as human science. Further evolution brought him to a humanist republicanism colored by elitist nostalgia and a belief in a "hidden God."

8. *arbitrary postulates of Sorel*: Georges Sorel (1847-1922), French social philosopher; originally a liberal conservative in his writings, he went on to a belief in a "free" Marxism, and then to revolutionary syndicalism, as exemplified in his best-known work, *Reflections on Violence* (1908 in French, and 1914 and 1950 in English translation). In this work, "violence" was linked to "myth." Paradoxically, he supported the French monarchist movement prior to World War I, and then supported the Leninist Bolsheviks in Russia in 1919.

Index

39
45 3 principles
47

48
5 a all available 52, 54, 55
5 8 The FOOL
6 0 average man
6 1 Barbarian norms.
80 Russian Rev,
84 new Common man,
85 autocratic life
95 mass man
98 Specialist!
108 effects of the state
109 The Harm of the State,
121 no one left to rule — rebellion
166 no one knows the way!
169 Individualism! Communism? NO